Girls and Sexuality

TEACHING AND LEARNING

Edited by Lesley Holly

Open University Press
Milton Keynes · Philadelphia

Open University Press
12 Cofferidge Close
Stony Stratford
Milton Keynes MK11 1BY

and
242 Cherry Street
Philadelphia, PA 19106, USA

First Published 1989

British Library Cataloguing in Publication Data

Girls and Sexuality: teaching and learning.
  1. Sex education – Role of schools
  I. Holly, Lesley   II. Series
  613.9′5071

  0–335–09532–1

Library of Congress Cataloging-in-Publication Data

Girls and sexuality : teaching and learning / edited by Lesley Holly.
     p.   cm.—(Gender and education)
   1. Sex instruction—Great Britain.   2. Girls—Great Britain—
Sexual behaviour .   I. Holly, Lesley.   II. Series: Gender and
education series.
HQ57.2.G57   1989
306.7′07′041—dc19   88–26836
                                                          CIP

Typeset by Colset (Pte.) Limited, Singapore
Printed in Great Britain by J.W. Arrowsmith Limited, Bristol

must be returned immed-
for by the Librarian,
the last date

OPEN UNIVERSITY PRESS

Gender and Education Series

Editors

ROSEMARY DEEM

*Senior Lecturer in the School of Education at the
Open University*

GABY WEINER

*Staff Tutor in the School of Education at the
Open University, London Region*

The series provides compact and clear accounts of relevant research
and practice in the field of gender and education. It is aimed at
trainee and practising teachers, and parents and others with an
educational interest in ending gender inequality. All age-ranges will
be included, and there will be an emphasis on ethnicity as well as
gender. Series authors are all established educational practitioners
or researchers.

TITLES IN THE SERIES

Boys Don't Cry
Sue Askew and Carol Ross

Untying the Apron Strings
Naima Browne and Pauline France (eds)

Changing Perspectives on Gender
Helen Burchell and Val Millman (eds)

Co-education Reconsidered
Rosemary Deem (ed.)

Women Teachers
Hilary De Lyon and Frances Widdowson Migniuolo (eds)

Girls and Sexuality
Lesley Holly (ed.)

Just a Bunch of Girls
Gaby Weiner (ed.)

Women and Training
Ann Wickham

Contents

Series Editor's Introduction

Recent government moves to assign sex education to that part of the school curriculum concerned with promoting the virtues of marriage and family life have, once again, brought sexuality and how it should be dealt with by teachers, to the forefront of the educational stage. In fact, as Lesley Holly points out in her introductory chapter, over the last decade sex education in one form or another has scarcely been off the front pages of the national and local press. The genuine attempts by the Greater London Council and some local educational authorities to acknowledge that many of their pupils will be gay or lesbian or that sexual harassment is a common occurrence in everyday classroom life, drew not only the to-be-expected shrill responses of the tabloid press, but a sustained campaign by the 'respectable' educational weeklies against what were termed as the antics of the 'loony left'.

This book, the eighth in the *Gender and Education* series, examines the unique place of sex in schooling; as a curriculum subject (viz sex and health education); as an indication of a specific process of accommodation and adjustment to social expectations (masculine or feminine behaviour); and as a set of distinctive experiences of school life (harassment, treatment by teachers and peers etc.). The contentious debate surrounding this topic has been responsible simultaneously for its marginality to the official business of schools, and indicative of the centrality of its importance to pupils and teachers alike. This selection of new articles reflecting the debates around sexuality and sex education in schooling of the late 1980s, for example on AIDS and child abuse, is organized around three themes – what is taught about sex and sexuality in school, the contradictions of being female in the day-to-day experiences of school life, and the features linking girls' and women's experience.

Important for all teachers, parents, school counsellors and others interested in knowing about the 'hidden' curriculum of schooling, this volume offers case studies of school experience, analyses of specific issues, and guidance about strategies and means of change. Not all will agree with the perspectives of all the authors. But none will fail to acknowledge the right to freedom of expression, the dangers of suppressing views which challenge official state policy (for instance on Clause 28) and the validity of the range of viewpoints offered.

Gaby Weiner

Acknowledgements

I should like to thank the following people for help with this book: the staff of the Cambridge Institute of Education Library, especially Betty Orange who directed me to many of the statistical sources used in this book and Angela Cutts for support and assistance with word processing; also Tony Booth for reading and commenting on earlier drafts of some of these chapters, Eileen O'Conner for typing and Gaby Weiner for support throughout.

Notes on Contributors

Lesley Holly collected the material for this book while working in the School of Education at the Open University. She is currently a tutor and researcher at the Institute of Education in Cambridge.

Lynda Measor was a research Fellow at the Open University for five years where she undertook the research for this chapter. She is now a senior lecturer in the Teaching Studies Department of the West Sussex Institute of Higher Education.

Jenny Kitzinger is a feminist who was involved in setting up the Cambridge Incest Survivors refuge. Her paid work has been in the Child Care and Development Group at the University of Cambridge and she is now working on the Sociological content of AIDS media messages at the Medical Sociology unit at Glasgow University.

Shirley Prendergast is a Senior Research Associate at the Child Care and Development Group at the University of Cambridge. She is currently writing a study of parenthood education in secondary schools, funded by the Health Education Authority. She has long been interested in the meaning of menstruation to young women, and will be following up the pilot study reported here in a full study, to be funded by the Health Promotion Research Trust, in 1989.

Isobel Gill is a pseudonym, a character in one of the author's plays, because apart from having fourteen years, experience of teaching in comprehensive schools the author is a poet and a playwright. One of the plays which she co-wrote, *The Memorial Garden*, was staged in London in spring 1988.

The Lesbian Mothers Group was started in 1984 and met for three years as a support group for mothers and their children.

Jacqui Halson is now teaching the Sociology of Deviance at the University of Kent at Canterbury. She previously lectured at Coventry Polytechnic and taught in Adult Education in Coventry and Leeds. She has a long standing interest in sexual violence (arising from living in Leeds during Peter Sutcliffe's reign of terror) which prompted her post graduate research, at Warwick University, on young women and the 'normalization' of sexual harassment.

CHAPTER 1

Introduction: The Sexual Agenda of Schools

LESLEY HOLLY

Three years ago events in my life made me begin to reconsider issues about sexuality in school. At that time my daughter left the relative security of the junior school to enrol as a student at a local comprehensive. Besides the tensions related to work and study there were all the other anxieties associated with emerging womanhood like menstruation and negotiating life in schools with adolescent boys.

My daughter's experiences evoked memories of my own school days in a mixed state secondary school; the nervous embarrassment when human reproduction was disscussed in biology lessons, the sexual references which we only half understood which were shouted out by boys as groups of girls cycled home from school, and of course the apprehension about menstruation. As I saw my daughter and her friends coping with these issues it occurred to me that millions of women have suffered the same anxieties.

At this time too, I was working as an assistant on a research project looking at management structures in schools. The research was mapped out by the male lecturers who directed the project. It would have been difficult not to notice that I was interviewing only a very small number of women from senior management. Increasingly I was also becoming aware of at least part of the context of male–female relations in schools – sexual harassment, graffiti and abusive language. Because of these issues the aims of the research project receded. Sitting in staffrooms, walking down school corridors, I developed my own agenda for study which came from my daughter's experiences and my own earlier ones.

As I interviewed male heads and male deputies in comprehensive schools on their ideas about school organization I often tried to raise issues with them about girls and women. I listened to one head

explaining about the role of the comprehensive in assisting all pupils
to fulfil their potential. After half an hour, when he paused for
breath, I asked him what happened to pregnant pupils in this school.
As an inner-city school this could not have been an unusual event
and it seemed to me that this was one group of pupils whose
educational potential might be left unfulfilled. Also I really wanted
to know the answer. The head ushered me out immediately and
referred me to a female head of year who told me that pregnant girls
stayed at home until the birth and could then return to another
school.

Reconsidering this incident later led me to explore some neglected
issues about women and sexuality. After all, why should male
embarrassment and silence limit and confine what can be discussed?
I was already uncomfortable about how my original research project had inflated the images of certain men thus decreasing the
visibility of women. I decided that at least in my own work concern
with women's lives should be a priority.

Therefore a major theme of this book is to make women's experience visible. Many of the authors are teachers and parents and they
write directly about their experience of schools and classrooms,
Some of the authors are researchers whose writing draws on interview material with teachers and pupils. There has been no attempt
to produce a synthesis of ideas but rather the aim has been to bring
certain issues to the attention of the reader in an immediate way, to
present contradictions which have not necessarily been resolved and
to discuss the diversity of experience which relates to sexuality.
Certainly sexuality is the hidden agenda running through nearly
every aspect of life and is always present in everyday relations
between the sexes. Learning about sexuality is therefore also learning about power relations between men and women. Understanding
these relations of power is central to this book.

The book has three main intentions. The first is to consider what
is taught about sex and sexuality in schools as part of the hidden
curriculum. What images of girls and women do schools reflect? The
second intention is to express some of the contradictions, tensions
and anxieties of being female in co-educational schools. The contri-
butors draw from a deep well of women's experiences which we
share but perhaps rarely discuss. The third intention is to make the
links between the different experiences of women and consider that
they may form a common oppression. Lesbian and heterosexual
women have shared interests in redefining sexual identities. A

predatory heterosexual environment ultimately works against the interests of all women.

A feminist agenda

These kinds of issues have been articulated through the women's movement over a long period and very effectively in the last twenty years. Consequently there has been an accelerating awareness of sexual inequality which has made some impact on our educational system as well as other areas of life. Some studies now exist of inequality and sexism in education which examine subjects like sex stereotyping in reading schemes or why girls are unwilling to opt for physics (Whyte 1986; Whyte *et al.* 1985). These issues are important because they are tangible signs of a system which discriminates on the basis of sex. In response to these debates there have been changes in the curriculum in many schools, so that there is probably less sexist language now and option schemes have been rethought.

However, these analyses of sexist practice and even the resulting changes in the curriculum are limited while they exclude a recognition of underlying power relations. Many changes in schools are cosmetic because deep issues about sexuality remain hidden. Of course it is not really hidden – sexuality is evident everywhere, in school and in everyday life. Furthermore over half the population menstruate between the ages of twelve and fifty-five. A majority of women experience pregnancy and childbirth. In a society where menstruation and pregnancy are considered a handicap, and social practices make sure that this is so, sexuality will remain the basis of domination between the sexes.

Catherine MacKinnon describes sexuality and what it means to feminists as 'that which is most one's own yet most taken away' (MacKinnon 1983, p. 277). This signals the intrusive nature of oppression through sexuality. The oppression may be a feature of personal relationships and certainly is a result of the public display of women's bodies through advertising and the media. This combination of the intimacy of personal relationships and the ways they enmesh with the sexual politics of the wider society has been a focal point for a feminist critique. A redefinition of sexuality which acknowledges women's sexual autonomy has been fundamental for the women's movement, as has the attempt to redeem a positive sexuality for women from a society which is deeply ambivalent towards women. The media appears to love women, and the celebration of women's bodies as page three pin-ups has become our accustomed diet of soft porn. The objects of this adulation are not women in general but young women. There is a deep distaste in our culture for the female body in all its phases of maturity. Girls and women who are menstruating, women during the menopause, older women are all subject to ridicule from a deep well of cultural misogyny. Meanwhile younger women feel compelled to produce themselves as copies of the current stereotype of female beauty.

Feminism has raised awareness of women's continuing oppression. Feminist writers have challenged pornography with its assumptions about women's constant availability as sexual objects for men. 'Rape Crisis' and 'Incest Survivors' groups have publicized the trauma of these experiences and organized support for women and girls. These initiatives have led to wider publicity. Certainly the more serious press and television often discuss women's issues and appear to take them seriously. However because anti-sexist policies do not exist in the press or television there are no standards by which all programmes or articles are judged. An article about rape may be one page away from holiday advertisements featuring semi-nude women. Similarly, television programmes raising issues about women's oppression may be set into an evening's viewing where sexual violence and pornography feature freely in other programmes. Britain's favourite newspaper shows little evidence of the awareness of feminism. It is depressing to realize that soft porn in combination with sentimental royalism and football still sells newspapers by the million.

Whatever the impact of feminism on the wider society it has certainly been influential in the lives of many women. Feminist ideas have encouraged some women to retrieve their sexuality from the confines of marriage and the family. This has often followed a rejection of cultural imperatives about what is natural and normal. The cornerstone of this normality is heterosexuality. As it is portrayed in our cultural myths, heterosexuality involves relationships between people who are not equals. The man in marriage is traditionally older than the woman. The chances of economic equality are slight. Marriage today often means she will relinquish her work to take care of him and the children, compounding her economic dependency even further. The heterosexual environment is not therefore a meeting of equals. It contains overtones of female dependency, female availability.

Sexuality in school

This is the atmosphere of our co-educational schools. Sexuality does
not remain outside the school gates. It is a constituent of life in
schools as it is of any other part of social life. The underlying sexual
dynamics of life in school are highly visible yet usually shrouded in
silence on the part of school authorities, which enables the expression of a certain kind of sexuality to appear normal, everyday and
unremarkable, echoing the attitudes of the rest of society. Sexual
harassment and abusive language are often accepted as ordinary life
in school.

During the socialist years of the Greater London Council, some of
the education authorities tried to raise issues about the heterosexual
environment of schools and some, like Ealing and Haringey,
brought out policy documents which were circulated in schools.
This attempt to raise awareness of sexuality in schools was met with
an extremely negative response on the part of some members of the
public mainly because of suggestions in the document that lesbian
and homosexual teachers should be able to be open about their
choices in school if they wished. A desire to have more open discussion in schools about homosexuality, especially in sex education, led
to accusations about 'gay lessons'. The ensuing bad publicity
crushed an important attempt to raise these issues.

Of course pupils unofficially learn about sexuality and its inter-
connections with power relations between the sexes. Although
many aspects of sexuality may be unacknowledged it remains a
resource on which pupils can draw to reinforce their sexual identity.
Boys can use sexual language to keep girls in their place. In this way
their masculinity is reinforced. Girls can respond to sexual stereotypes by rejecting them or quietly living with passive femininity for
an easy life. Teachers can also draw on sexuality in their relations
with pupils. Given the inequalities which underlie all male–female
relations, this is an especially potent source of power for male
teachers dealing with younger women and girls. There is always the
possibility of relating through sexuality and encouraging young
women to do so in return. The effect of these sexualized encounters
is to reproduce the idea of male superiority.

Most of these sexualized exchanges in schools are hidden in the
classroom away from the possibility of any public discussion.
Sometimes, however, schools are forced to respond to incidents
which are overtly sexual. Any staff–pupil relationship which

moves beyond sexual banter might warrant intervention. Usually, however, the intervention concerns relationships outside school. Supporting a teenage pregnancy or dealing with child abuse might be part of the pastoral care system. Sexual harassment usually has to reach the level of violent attack before it is noticed.

Of course sexuality is not just the hidden agenda of schooling. It is part of the school curriculum in that there are rules which regulate sexuality and the ways it can be represented or expressed in school. These rules often concern uniform or dress and always include school facilities such as the use of changing rooms or cloakrooms (Prendergast and Prout 1987, p. 233).

Sex education

Sex education may start in the junior school as part of the taught curriculum but is more routinely included in the curriculum in the secondary school, though not necessarily in special schools (see Chapter 2). Teaching about sex is usually underpinned by a view of normal relations between the sexes. This normality includes heterosexuality and polarized gender roles (and these are of course reflected in the organization and management structure of the school). Prendergast and Prout (1985) discuss how sex education is introduced in the first two years in secondary school. There is usually a review of facts including information on puberty and menstruation. Their study of sex and parenthood education in secondary schools suggests that by the fourth year sex education is situated in a more personal framework. The emphasis, however, is on reproduction, contraception and disease. This is discussed by Isobel Allen in her recent review of sex education. She comments on the 'shock horror' approach in some schools (1987, p. 63). Sex is seen as dangerous, especially for young women who are often seen as sexual victims. The emphasis in school on giving information may mean that there is very little time to discuss the personal responses of young people to sex. Many pupils interviewed for the recent survey (Allen *op. cit.*) felt that there was no space for discussions about feelings and emotion. This must mean that although sex is on the agenda in sex education courses, sexuality is often left out. If women are not to be the passive objects of male sexuality then there needs to be the space to consider sexual feelings and sexual desire. This might give young women the chance both to understand wider issues about

sexuality and to discuss their own needs and desires for sexual relationships. Sex is very powerful behaviour in our society and it is
unlikely it will be given up despite images of terror. Shirley
Prendergast has suggested that at the moment we have the worst of
both worlds. Young people go on having sexual relations in situations of risk and they are terrified (personal communication, May
1988). This suggestion also emerged from Michelle Fine's research in
New York schools. She suggests that young women are vulnerable
because there is no space to discuss sexual feelings and emotions.

> The adolescent woman herself assumes a dual consciousness – at
> once taken with the excitement of actual anticipated sexuality and
> consumed with anxiety and worry. While too few safe spaces exist for
> adolescent women's explorations of sexual subjectivities there are all
> too many dangerous spots for their exploitation. (Fine 1988, p. 35)

Giving young women a chance to discuss issues about sexuality
could be important in moving away from a victim approach to sex
education.

Recently the Conservative government has encouraged teachers
to situate sex education within the context of the morality of marriage
and the family. The 1986 Education Act even allows school governors to ban sex education. Moreover, the 1988 Local Government
Act outlaws the 'promotion' of homosexuality by local authorities,
and obviously this could be applied to sex education in schools. As a
consequence, many vital issues will be dealt with in an inadequate
way. The number of cases of some sexually transmitted diseases are
increasing. It may be true that limiting one's sexual experiences to
one partner for life may decrease the risks of catching sexually
transmitted diseases. However, it is clear from divorce statistics that
most relationships do not last for life.[1] Most people do have more
than one sexual partner. Sex education should surely prepare pupils
for the life they are most likely to live. Yet in the current climate it
seems all too likely that sex education courses will become even
more limited.

What is in this book?

The first section

The subject matter of this book is sexuality and how it should be
taught and discussed in schools. What changes are necessary to

make schools into environments where women and girls can feel comfortable and accepted? The first section is called 'What should we teach about sex?' The chapters in this section raise questions about the ways sex is taught in schools asking what issues should be included and how they should be discussed. In the first chapter teachers of sex education write about the underlying commitments and values which influence their teaching. They discuss the desirability of teaching single-sex groups and the relevance of situating sex education within a family context.

There follows a chapter based on conversations and discussions with young women about AIDS (HIV virus) and other sexually transmitted diseases. How do they regard their present and future sexual relationships? The next chapter by Lynda Measor points to the disparity between the development of adolescent sexual aware-ness and sex education courses. She writes about the confrontation between adolescents' experience of the world and the sex education classes which they are forced to attend.

Increasingly children in junior school receive sex education which focuses on sexual abuse and how to avoid it. There are programmes in some junior schools in which both pupils and teachers are encouraged to participate. Jenny Kitzinger looks at these programmes and the teacher's role when trying to support abused children.

The final chapter in this section asks what happens when, in its own terms, sex education fails? If pupils do not use appropriate contraception and a teenage girl gets pregnant what can she expect from the education system as a schoolgirl mother?

The second section

In the second section 'Reflecting on our experiences', pupils, parents, teachers and researchers discuss the experience of being female in our mixed schools. How is women's sexuality reflected by schools? Not unexpectedly some of the answers to this question include dis-cussions about silence, embarrassment, misunderstanding, and sexual harassment.

This section looks at the environment of schools to discuss how heterosexual normality can be quite oppressive for girls. Some of these concerns would not be included in the formal curriculum but genuine moves towards anti-sexist education must include an awareness of these issues. Shirley Prendergast's chapter on menstruation begins this section. It is clear from her study that many of the difficulties and embarrassments of menstruation in school are unnecessarily maintained by school organization and often fostered by unsympathetic sexist staff attitudes. The next chapter by Isobel Gill describes her life as a white lesbian teacher in a boys' school. She was responsible for drawing up equal opportunities guidelines for her school and she decided to move away from 'the blandness' of this project and produced instead an 'anti-sexist, anti-heterosexist' document which directly raised many of the issues we are concerned with in this book.

This is followed by a chapter by a lesbian mothers group who discuss the support needed for their children coming from backgrounds which challenge society's ideas about 'normal' sexuality. This normality often includes the predatory sexuality which manifests inside and outside schools as sexual harassment. In the final chapter Jacqui Halson describes her research into the experiences of harassment in the lives of young women.

The chapters in this book raise issues about the teaching of sex education and the sexual agenda of schools which girls and women as pupils, teachers, parents and researchers have found important. They reflect on some ways in which women's sexuality is distorted, neglected or rejected, made invisible or repackaged to fit a male fantasy. We suggest that not only do schools reflect the sexuality of the wider society but they are deeply implicated in its maintenance.

Note

1 Over one-third of all marriages now end in divorce. *Social Trends* 18, HMSO, 1988.

Bibliography

Allen, I. (1987) *Education in Sex and Personal Relationships*. Policy Studies Institute.

Fine, M. (1988) Sexuality, Schooling and Adolescent Females: The Missing Discourse of Desire. *Harvard Educational Review* Vol. 5 No. 1.

MacKinnon, C. (1983) 'Feminism, Marxism Method and the State: An agenda for theory', in E. Abel and E. Abel (eds), *The Signs Reader*, University of Chicago Press.

Prendergast, S. and Prout, A. (1987) 'Smile at him when you ask for the books', in T. Booth and D. Coulby (eds) *Producing and Reducing Disaffection*, Open University Press.

Prendergast, S. and Prout, A. (1985) *Knowing and Learning about Parenthood*, Report of Education for Parenthood Project Mimeo. H.E.C. Library.

Whyte, J. (1986) *Girls into Science and Technology*, Routledge and Kegan Paul.

Whyte, J., Deem, R., Kant L. and Cruickshank, M. (1985) *Girl Friendly Schooling*, Methuen.

What Should We Teach About Sex?

CHAPTER 2

Teaching Sex: The Experiences of Four Teachers

LESLEY HOLLY

Teaching sex is a difficult job. In a pluralistic society, like Britain, it is unlikely that any consensus could exist about what should be included in sex education in schools. However, recent opinion polls do seem to indicate that a majority of parents support sex education as part of the curriculum. A Policy Studies Institute poll for the Family Planning Association in 1986 showed that 96 per cent of parents questioned thought that schools should provide some sex education. Although this parental support for sex education indicates that *something* should be taught it does not solve the problems of what, how and at which age. Indeed there are any number of pitfalls and however a course is tackled there will be critics among the parents.

Recently teachers of sex education have found themselves in an increasingly precarious situation. The spread of the HIV virus and the rise in the number of cases of many other sexually transmitted diseases have made the dissemination of information an urgent matter. The AIDS campaign has been directed towards raising public awareness and has presented the issues in easily accessible language to alert adults and young people. The problem for teachers is that the information is not neutral. Issues cannot necessarily be discussed in the same way inside school and outside school and once inside the school building it is not clear how to discuss emotive subjects such as safe sex, safe contraception and homosexuality.

Fears of moral laxity associated with the spread of the HIV virus have contributed to a new willingness to regard homosexuality with alarm. Before the demise of the Inner London Education Authority, education authorities within it such as Haringey and Ealing developed policies 'to overcome prejudice against homosexuality' and the

Ealing policy document suggested that 'education . . . involves encouraging respect for and acceptance of others' (1987). These initiatives were sensationalized by certain elements of the press as 'Gay lessons'. With the passing of Clause 28 in the Local Government Bill, no local authority may 'intentionally promote homosexuality'.

This will undoubtedly mean that it will be difficult for teachers to give even a factual explanation of homosexuality in schools. Martin Stafford suggests that the lesbian and gay 'positive images' initiatives were not a decline into 'moral nihilism' as some opponents fear. The idea that homosexuals and lesbians can form loving, responsible relationships can be accommodated in the existing moral values of our society. However, the chances of discussing those issues in the classroom has become an increasingly remote possibility. (Stafford 1988).

Unfortunately an emphasis on disease, responsibility and contraception does also leave out the idea that sexuality can be a source of happiness and enjoyment. Most young people in sex education classes already experience themselves as sexual beings in the widest sense. Locating sex education in the context of the family and safe sex will not necessarily provide space for understanding personal issues about sexuality and desire. This is especially important for young women if they are not merely to feel like passive victims of male sexuality.

Teachers of sex education are caught in a dilemma. The climate of Conservatism makes certain subjects difficult to teach and yet those may be the very issues which pupils most need to consider. Clearly what to include and how to present sex education courses lies at the heart of the debate. Until recently the way issues have been woven together has been the responsibility of the teacher in the classroom. Now, the 1986 Education Act is intended as an intervention in this process, suggesting that family life should be emphasized in sex education. It states:

> . . . Where sex education is given . . . it is given in such a manner as
> to encourage those pupils to have due regard to moral considerations
> and the value of family life.
>   (Education Act, No. 2, 1986, Section 531, No. 7)

Furthermore, school governors will have the right to preview books and materials to be used in sex education lessons, to criticize the course, and even to veto all sex education in their school. Speaking

at the Conservative Party conference in October 1986 the Secretary
for Education, Kenneth Baker, said:

> Control over sex education will be removed from teachers and local
> authorities and given to the governing bodies.

What do teachers say about teaching sex education?

Most teachers designing sex education courses come to decisions
about content and presentation after a process of discussion with
colleagues and parents. Inevitably, however, the course reflects
teachers' commitment to providing what pupils need to know to
preserve their health and safety in the modern world and come to
some understanding about their own sexuality.

In this chapter, four teachers write about how they present sex
education lessons. They all approach the issues from different
standpoints and according to the different needs of their pupils. All
are convinced that sex education is essential and have arrived at
their particular courses after debate, discussion and often considerable anxiety. All four teachers find situating sex within marriage and
the family problematic for similar reasons.

Ruth Quilter

*Ruth Quilter teaches in a college of further education. She works on
three-year courses with students with severe learning difficulties
who go to the college when they are sixteen. She has also taught sex
education to women from the Adult Training Centre, who are aged
between twenty-five and forty, and mixed groups of adults from the
local sub-normality hospital. Sex education is only a part of her
work, a part which has caused her concern and anxiety, but she
remains convinced of its importance.*

Society has been prepared to deny the knowledge of sexuality to
mentally handicapped people with severe learning difficulties. It is
something most of us would rather not think about and if we are
forced to think about it we really do not like it. For this reason as
much as any other, mentally handicapped people are not comfortable with their own bodies. They do not have a good body image.
Often their sexuality is quite dormant. Therefore you have to work
carefully when discussing sex.

At the college where I work we decided we had to teach sex

education, although often special schools will not teach it. I know this because I have taught in four special schools and not one had a sex education programme. Colleges of further education take it more seriously because pupils are in an integrated environment and girls, especially, are 'at risk'. A major concern for pupils with special needs in our college is developing independence so, for instance, we want them to go to the coffee bar at lunch time. They are going to be on their own there with all the other students and we have got to be sure we are giving them enough knowledge in all sorts of areas to enable them to cope. Sex education is part of that.

Once we had committed ourselves to initiating it, staff who were involved in teaching sex education went on training courses. That is important, because so many of the issues it raises are personal, which you have to address before you can discuss sex with young people. And we worked with parents. I do not know if they were typical but they were a courageous group of parents and they responded by saying, 'Yes. We've got to do this.' We had sessions with parents where we broke into groups and discussed what should be in the curriculum. Eventually it came down to us taking a deep breath and going into the classroom, knowing we had got parental support.

It is easier for me as a woman to talk to girls. My male colleague teaches the boys. When I put the programme together I wanted to ensure that I was opening the way for these girls to have some knowledge of their own sexuality as opposed to a received sexuality. I think a lot of women suffer from the idea that sex is about penetration and that masturbation for women is more problematic or less acceptable than it is for men. Trying to describe what a clitoris is, is quite difficult. I do not think my male colleague could have tackled this subject in the same direct way. I do not think the girls would have found it easy to accept from him. They did not find it very easy with me.

The course I teach is a life cycle approach – from birth until death – and sexuality is put into that context. The curriculum can be broadened wherever it is appropriate. It is not just about sex in a nuts and bolts way but about emotions, responsibility, body awareness, choices. A lot of the work involves building up trust and becoming easy with words. The communication difficulties that some pupils have, the difficulties with grasping concepts, dealing with feelings, makes it harder for severely mentally handicapped women.

When we got to menstruation we talked about what it is and how to cope with it. Some girls wanted to continue to swim when they had their period as they knew I did. We actually had a session when we all tried to put in tampons, in the teaching bathroom. There was no pressure on them to do it, but if they wanted to I let them try it out.

Also we had sessions where we went into town and I said, 'Your task is to buy a packet of sanitary towels.' 'Now where do we start?' 'Can you recognize them on the shelf?' 'How much do they cost?' So I was aiming to give these young women the independence to know how to take care of themselves.

We went through sexuality and described what sexual intercourse is, which can take months and months of work. In the broadest sense it is also about morality. I do not mean in the 'it's wrong to have sex before marriage' sense, but how to treat other people and how to take care of ourselves as women.

We went on to the questions: Marriage or not marriage? Sex or not sex? This is a recognition that sexual intercourse is not an obligatory part of a relationship. It is a personal choice. I tried to emphasize this in my approach and I said, 'You do not have to do this. This is what quite a lot of people do and some enjoy it. A lot of people do not do it and this is quite all right.' I did not want them to feel that sex is what 'normal' people do, so they had to do it regardless of whether they were mature enough or not.

They really enjoyed the work on childbirth and children. They always wanted to see the film of a woman giving birth twice. Then we moved on to contraception. It was difficult for them to grasp the idea of their 'insides'. Diagrams do not always mean much. Trying to describe how the pill works is hard. It is important to cover the basics, and we can always go back over the subject another year. The girls need to understand that there are ways of not having children and the purpose and location of family planning clinics.

We do not cover all these issues with *all* the students, because not all the students are ready. We might do relationships, naming of parts, menstruation in one term. Then students might be put into different groups if some things are thought not to be relevant – like sexually transmitted diseases, for example. The groups do not relate to age but to maturity and need. The course spans three years so there is time to come back.

For me, there are still many more questions than there are answers. Is it relevant for all of them? How do you successfully teach the broader issues? How do you evaluate what the students have learnt? I sometimes felt anxious about how I had taught a particular subject or concept.

I remember I had taught one group about sexual intercourse and I went back over it and said, 'Now what comes out of a man's penis?' and Karen, one of my girls, said, 'A mouse.' I thought, 'What have I done? What are these girls getting from me?' Then Karen said, 'No, no a fish.' She meant that we had talked about sperm being like little fishes, but she had got it into a category of little animals and so she had come up with a mouse.

We will never have all the answers, but you plan as much as possible, try it out and then revise your plans. I believe this is a very important part of these students' education and it is vital that we tackle the subject of sex and personal relationships – even if it is difficult. For the students, it has got to be better than being left in ignorance.

Renee Swetman

Until recently Renee Swetman taught a sex education course to fourth year pupils in a large mixed rural comprehensive. This is part of a two-year health education course which also covers such issues as smoking and drugs. Personal and emotional issues are prominent.

I inherited a course that had already been written so the framework was there. When I became responsible for that area I modified it slightly. I thought it was quite sound and I just introduced some new material.

We taught health education as a team – sixty students and three members of staff – so it had to be quite well structured. Sometimes people allocated to teach health education were not familiar with the area or relaxed about teaching it. Often I took the large group and then we split into discussion groups. Ideally I think you should leave a lot of the teaching to spontaneous exploration of issues and be prepared to let things move in the direction of the group that you are with at the time. However, if teachers are anxious this is not possible and then there must be more structure to the discussions.

We started the first session by getting the group to work in a slightly different way from other lessons, sitting round informally rather than behind desks. The aim of that first session was to get people to relax and feel that they were going to have an opportunity to look at things that were relevant to them. Then the course was explained and we said we recognized that if at any stage any of them wanted to ask anything it might be hard for them to ask directly and it was appropriate to write their question down on paper anonymously.

The first stumbling block (and I am sure most teachers who are involved in sex education find this) was the whole question of language – using a common language. If you start talking about 'sexual intercourse', or 'making love', that really is not relevant to a lot of pupils. The way I tried to overcome it was by brainstorming. I would say, 'sexual intercourse, how many other words do you know for it?' I would write the words on the board so they were visible. It stopped pupils disrupting the lessons because it was all open and acknowledged and words were available to be used.

Everything was taught in mixed groups except for a session on contraception. The whole group was shown a film on contraception and initially they split into mixed-sex groups but it was quite clear that everyone was very inhibited. The boys made fun of all the different contraceptives. The girls were just frozen by it. It worked much better in single-sex groups. The Health Education Council provides kits of all contraceptives. I think there is a lot of value in seeing everything. Girls of fourteen or fifteen often want contraception, but since the 'Gillick'[1] ruling they are terrified of going to their GP. For the girls who were having sex at fourteen this was valuable information.

Things came out in the written questions. If important issues did not come up in questions we would pretend that they had so that we explored every issue. There was a film which said, 'Boys sometimes masturbate and this is normal.' If anything about masturbation was asked, even if the question was not directed at girls or women, we always talked about women masturbating as well. I think many of them really appreciated it. There were no giggles or anything like that. People genuinely wanted to know. Many girls had never had anyone talk about their body, and it was quite clearly a subject which was not understood.

Another issue that was raised was about love making. A lot of girls are still very much into boosting the male ego and they do not often have the chance to talk about anything like the need to fake orgasm or pretend it was all right. What expectations could one have of sex? Are they realistic? I'm sure it's an area that could be talked about a lot more but it needs a safe environment of a girls-only group.

In my teaching group I did not push my views too strongly unless asked. Throughout the sex education course pupils did ask my opinions and then I always gave them honestly. The person I worked with, it seemed to me, was always presenting the moral line of 'This won't happen to you if you don't sleep around'. When this teacher got asked if he had ever had VD he was outraged and got hot and blustery. After he had finished what he had got to say, I said that I had attended a clinic with a minor sexually transmitted disease. I diffused the tension. It felt important to say it then.

Some issues are contentious in a school environment – homosexuality for example. If you are going to deal with these issues, as you should, you have to make sure you have the support of the head – otherwise you could take all the backlash from parents. Some young people I see now that I used to teach are homosexuals or lesbians. They did not feel that they were able to say it at school.

Pam Towns

Pam Towns teaches in a girls' comprehensive in a new town. She is a science teacher and sex education is taught as part of the science curriculum in the second year. This is a factual approach to sex education. Emotional aspects are covered in a personal and social relationships course in the fourth year. Inevitably there is an overlap and Pam deals with emotional issues in the second year as well.

I teach in a girls-only school and pupils are very open because they are not embarrassed by the presence of boys. Some are not very mature. They often have had very little experience of the opposite sex. I think that they resolve their problems better as girls but perhaps they do not know what all their problems are.

In the second year, sex education is a nuts and bolts approach. It is a forum for questions and answers – a debriefing of their myths and prejudices and an explanation of the mechanics of what actually goes on. In the fourth year they are discussing sex in personal and social relationships classes in a less theoretical and more emotional way. I think the fourth year is the right time to start to do that although many are already sexually active by then.

My approach throughout is that I tend to be a horror merchant. I think it very important they should know that they may be messing up, not only their emotions, but their bodies too. I think that these girls should take more responsibility for every aspect of their life. I believe most boys are less likely to take responsibility and therefore girls must, because pregnancy and most sexually transmitted diseases do not have the same effects on men's lives.

When I am teaching about sexually transmitted diseases, including HIV, I work through the medical aspects and then get them to consider how these diseases might affect their lives and how this relates to their ability to say 'no' to sex. Does it make the fact that they can not do it more worrisome? This is a problem for someone who has grown up without love and finds it difficult to say 'no'. Quite a few girls are in that position. You have to try to let them build strategies to cope with that as much as any other aspect.

When I teach contraception I explain the medical advantages of the condom, how it helps to avoid the HIV virus and cervical cancer. I tend to talk about their own bodies – I try not to give a moral view just basic information. Despite all the teaching you will always get pregnant schoolgirls. The AIDS epidemic may eventually cause a drop in teenage pregnancies, but there will always be the one. It does not matter how much contraceptive advice you give them, they will not use contraceptives because they want the baby as much as anything. It is going to be their own. Their only source of true love.

I do not site sex education in the family. You are talking to a mixed audience where there are children from one-parent families, children in care, children in foster homes – children that are not in a nuclear family – and I think that it is insulting to deal in that kind of framework. It gives them hang-ups. Homosexuality rarely comes up in my class. If I get a question about it I usually approach it through the idea that we are all individuals and this may not be right for you but it may be right for someone else, and you really have to respect other people's way of life. Again it goes back to not giving the family view. You may have the girl who lives with her mother while her father is homosexual and overtly so, and it would be wrong to put her against her father. So I try to give an open view on all of that.

Norma Neeson

Norma Neeson is a member of the Humanities department in a small comprehensive. She teaches sex education as part of her work in a health education course which she designed. This course gives information about sex and raises issues about relationships, as well as covering such subjects as disability, third world poverty and health issues.

The fourth years start off with a term on health and sex education. They didn't have that at this school before I went there. They did some work in biology, but not all the pupils do biology and I felt that everyone at that age should know about contraceptives, VD, AIDS, drugs, alcohol – all of that. They are mixed classes. I have asked pupils whether they would prefer single-sex classes but I am not the only person who teaches sex education so I have to negotiate. Also I want to make sure boys see things from the girls' point of view.

When I do contraception, I try to be very relaxed and I try not to make it too clinical. I show them all the different contraceptives – I feel very strongly that the boys should see all the things that women have to do to stop them having children. They can write down any questions and they are always basically the same ones.

One of the main themes I am concerned about at the moment is people being pushed into sexual relationships earlier than they actually want to be, because there is peer-group pressure. I discuss comments boys might make – if the girl does she's a 'slut', if the girl doesn't she's 'frigid' – and I tell girls they should not give in to these sorts of comments. I never say you should only have sex within marriage although I know that there are people on the staff who feel I ought to. I say that it should be a decision you are happy about, that you are not going to regret later, and that your first and subsequent sexual experiences should be ones that are good for you, that are not worrying because you are thinking either that you might get pregnant or catch the HIV virus or that you do not feel you really like this person, or that they do not really like you. It should not be something you do because you are drunk and somebody is pressurizing you. And I know that girls feel a lot of pressure and I think that many more have earlier, and earlier sexual experience. When I was at school some pupils would be having sex around fifteen. That age has come down and I am convinced it is because of pressure. It worries me. I do not think some girls actually take much part in the decision, they acquiesce.

Although I have done it for a few years I still find sex education a difficult subject to teach and although I hope I am relaxed and confident in the classroom it remains difficult because of its very personal nature and because, for most pupils, sex is an unknown area except for ideas which have been formulated from the hype and romanticism which the media churns out. The one thing I would do, if I had enough money, would be to buy each of them a copy of *Make It Happy* by Jane Cousins which is a book for young teenagers about sex. It talks about orgasm, it talks about every single aspect of sex, the law and sex, contraception, everything. I recommend it to them.

Postscript

Although the emphasis may be different, these four teachers all prioritize teaching sex in a clear and accessible way – both the perils and some of the pleasures. They all appreciate how information about contraception and sexually transmitted diseases constitutes an essential survival kit for all young people in our society.

The slogan 'Don't Die of Ignorance' featured in the AIDS campaign indicates that the Conservative government also knows that information saves lives. However, the recent education bill indicates a pernicious double standard. The right to information about the potential hazards of sexual encounters applies outside the classroom but not within it. School Governors may now decide whether sex education is taught and how it is taught. Pupils' needs, for information which will help them to make decisions about their lives, are given low priority as opposed to governors' rights to control information. If pupils are allowed the information, the bill suggests it must be enclosed in the morality of the family. This approach will make sex education less accessible to many young people. They require information which relates directly to their present circumstances. The morality of the family cannot guarantee protection for a sexually active teenage population from pregnancy or the HIV virus or any other sexually transmitted disease.

Although none of these teachers situate sex education within a setting encouraging marriage and family life, they all argue for a morality based on self-respect. This is the most appropriate approach to sex education. Anything else is surely patronizing and unrealistic and may lead pupils to ignore, or dismiss as irrelevant, information which could save their lives, and stop them becoming aware of how to make their own decisions about sex.

Note

1 This controversial ruling forbids GPs to prescribe the contraceptive pill to girls under sixteen without notifying their parents.

Bibliography

Cousins, J. (1980) *Make it Happy – What sex is all about*, Penguin.

Education Act (No. 2) (1986) Section 531, No. 7, Butterworths.

London Borough of Ealing: Education Committee (1987) *Policy Statement on Sexual Equality*, January.

Stafford, J. M. (1988) 'In defence of gay lessons', *Journal of Moral Education*, Vol. 17, No. 1, January.

CHAPTER 3

'It makes you think again.' Discussing AIDS* and Other Sexually Transmitted Diseases

LESLEY HOLLY

Sexually transmitted diseases are on the increase. Over the past two years it has been the spread of the HIV virus which has monopolized space in the media and drawn the greatest concern. Aware that delay might lead to a greater loss of life, the government launched an advertising campaign to try to change some aspects of current sexual behaviour. As part of this campaign leaflets were sent to every household.

While not denying the rightness of this response, it does throw into sharp relief the inadequate level of publicity about other sexually transmitted diseases, many of which have very serious consequences for women. Information can help to prevent the spread of most sexually transmitted diseases. Is this information available to young women who are becoming sexually active especially in heterosexual relationships? Has the AIDS campaign itself had an impact on the young people it was intended to influence?

I talked to sixth-form girls in Milton Keynes to discuss these issues. The material in this chapter is drawn from conversations with ten sixth-form girls over a number of lunchtime sessions. The chapter addresses two major issues. First, what do these sixth-form girls know about the HIV virus and other sexually transmitted diseases? Second, what information do they need to know in order

---

*Because the HIV virus is generally known as AIDS it was referred to as such throughout these discussions.

to make informed choices? Then I suggest that there are important gaps in their knowledge which could leave them more vulnerable than necessary to catching sexually transmitted diseases. However, whatever information is given it cannot simply be part of sex education which equates sex with disease and risks. There has to be an acknowledgement that all information is weighed against a desire and need for sexual relationships.

I advertised some lunchtime discussion groups for young women in a school where I was working as a researcher. Ten young women, all sixth formers, replied. I did not ask them whether they were sexually active (nor did they ask me!) although it emerged from the discussion that some of them were. One of the young women was clearly assessing her sexual identity. The others considered themselves heterosexual. Because of the vulnerable position of the one young woman, sexual identity did not become an issue in these discussions.

What do you know about AIDS?

Because of the subject matter everyone was rather tongue-tied and embarrassed. Fortunately after about ten minutes they forgot to be self-conscious and we began by discussing the AIDS publicity. How did these girls find out about AIDS? Where did they get their information? Was it through the school? The consensus of opinion was that the school had played some part in informing pupils about AIDS. They had shown a film to fifth and sixth formers. There had been a talk which gave facts and figures although it had not been compulsory to attend.

Norma pointed out that the school was in a difficult position. 'People kick up a fuss when the school just tells us the basic facts of life. How are they going to tell us about AIDS? I think they have done sufficient.'

Kate suggested that information came from a number of sources, including school, and informal conversations with friends. 'Before the leaflet came through the door I knew what it was. How to catch it, I learnt that at school (before the government did anything about it) from television programmes, chatting, people coming into school, before the leaflet or anything.'

Most influential have been programmes on the television where pop stars pass on information about AIDS. All the girls I've spoken to saw these programmes.

> *Norma*: It's like a big club that everyone has joined, watching television programmes about AIDS with Bob Geldof and people on the telly making it very pally.

The girls agreed that these programmes were more successful in raising awareness than the advertisements. The latter came in for some criticism. It was suggested that advertisements do not give enough information.

> *Abigail*: The posters don't bother to explain what AIDS is or how you can catch it. There are all the slogans like 'Don't die of ignorance'.
> *Kate*: No. Adverts are no good at all.

But Kate remembered that the advertisements about AIDS encouraged her 'nan' to find out about it.

> I was surprised when I saw the adverts. I thought, 'This is not doing what it should do.' I thought, 'I know what it is because I've had someone tell me but my mum won't know, my nan won't know for definite.' Then one of the adverts came on the telly. My nan said, 'Do you know about that?' and she'd read about it and she knew all about it. It was really surprising. I didn't know that she knew. She didn't find out from the advert. She saw it and thought, 'What's that?' and went away and found out.

Lara was surprised that Kate's nan was in a high risk group!

> *Lara*: Is your nan likely to get AIDS?
> *Kate*: I don't think so. Old age is more likely to get her before AIDS does.

Although they felt that the programmes about AIDS were successful in raising awareness, the girls did not see the irony in having them in an evening's viewing when casual sex would undoubtedly be portrayed. They did not believe that television programmes themselves needed to change in the way they portrayed sexual behaviour.

> *Sally*: There are so many ways of showing sex-dramas, documentaries.
> *Norma*: I don't think it's harmful.

Some of the girls hardly noticed the sexual agenda of some of the programmes.

Mandy: Things like *Dynasty* and *Dallas*. There's not much casual sex
   is there?
Debbie: JR gets around a lot.
Sonia: You don't see a boob anywhere do you?

As the manipulation of sexuality lies at the heart of *Dallas* and
Dynasty the girls showed some naivety in failing to understand this.
By equating sexual promiscuity with nudity the constant atmosphere of sexual availability which sells *Dynasty* and *Dallas* is
misunderstood. This misunderstanding arises because the production and promotion of sexual images underpins our culture. It
is normal. Of course while sexual availability continues to be so
strongly promoted through the media the cultural encouragement
for promiscuity exists so the HIV virus may continue to spread.

Different . . . from our parents

There was considerable disagreement and ambivalence about what
kind of changes in behaviour might be necessary now AIDS is a
threat. However, the girls did believe that they would not lead the
same sexual lives as past generations.

Kate: It will definitely be different from what our parents went
   through at our age. Definitely.
Abigail: We've got this other threat hanging over us. As well as
   getting pregnant we can catch AIDS. It's not just pregnancy, it's
   death.
Sonia: Pregnancy is quite insignificant.

Marilyn and Sally suggested that some people will still have casual
sex, but they will be aware of the risks.

Marilyn: Casual sex will still go on but people may take more precautions. They're going to be aware of it. Everybody's got to be aware
   of it now.
Sally: People will still be promiscuous. It won't stop people having
   sex but just make them be a bit more aware of which partners they
   choose. I don't think it's so frightening that it's going to stop people
   completely.

So if 'other people' are likely to go on being promiscuous, how will
the threat of AIDS affect the future of the girls here? They admit that
they will be worried.

Mandy: It will worry me. It is always in the back of my mind.
Lara: I think it makes you think again. But then if you were sensible you'd be thinking about it anyway.
Abigail: It's brought something else to light hasn't it? Something else you've got to think about all the time.

Even with this level of concern some girls did not believe their chances of catching it were very great.

Abigail: I don't think there is too much risk at the moment but if people carry on having casual sex it will multiply rapidly.

Sharon suggests that the area where you live is an important factor when considering the risks of catching AIDS.

I think the risk really depends on what areas you live in. Where the level of prostitution is high and a lot of people have got AIDS . . . but I don't know. I can't see it coming to me here apart from the fact that I've got a steady boyfriend anyway, but even if I didn't I don't think I'm in a very high risk group. London, Birmingham where they have drugs – those are problem areas.

AIDS is all you ever hear about

Most publicity about sexually transmitted disease (STDs) has concentrated on the HIV virus. However there are other diseases which are spreading through the population, some of which are merely inconvenient, others can be fatal. The girls were not well informed. Kate summed this up by saying: 'AIDS is all you ever hear about.'
They had dealt with all sexually transmitted diseases in sex education classes but could not immediately think of any information about others apart from AIDS.

Marilyn: This all seems more remote. AIDS seems like the real threat.
Mandy: Syphilis and gonorrhoea seem very old fashioned now.

This lack of information is unfortunate as genital herpes and the human papilloma virus (genital warts) are escalating and they affect the sexes differently. They are a nuisance to men but the effect on women of catching these viruses can be far more serious.

'If it's a serious relationship you don't have to worry.'

The girls agreed that a responsible attitude was essential in future sexual relations and that was a way of protecting their health against sexually transmitted diseases. However for all these young women there was a conflict between wanting to establish sexual relationships and fears about catching sexually transmitted diseases. One way out of this problem was to consider their sexuality in terms of responsibility and serious relationships.

> *Debbie*: I think it depends a lot on what sort of person you are . . . I think for sensible people it's not an issue.
> *Norma*: If you mix with people who value themselves and value others and care, then it's avoidable.

This means that sex would be limited to 'serious relationships'.

> *Debbie*: If it's a serious relationship you don't have to worry.

The idea of the 'serious relationship' is one which triggers off a great deal of discussion. Norma suggests that being in love implies trust.

> *Norma*: When you love somebody you've got to trust them. By that time you'll know if someone's got AIDS or anything else.

Kate suggests the return of some old-fashioned virtues. 'Trust might become more important, I think. Faithfulness between two people might be more important than it is at the moment. I think people are going to be wary of AIDS. I will be.'

Somehow 'love' and 'serious relationships' are seen as defences against AIDS and other sexually transmitted diseases. This allows the young women to experience sexual desire without being terrified and without having to resort to condoms. They believe that there are ways of having sexual relationships which are safe.

At lunchtime we have conversations about 'condoms'.

How do these young women view the campaign to use condoms? Certainly 'condom' has become part of everyday conversation and this in turn seems to have generated more openness about sexuality.

> *Norma*: What makes me laugh is you've got the whole sixth form, probably the whole fifth form, who now say 'condoms' freely. Nobody would say it before. Nobody knew words for it. Now at lunchtime we have conversations about condoms.

Kate is aware of the changing politics of contraception. 'When we had sex education at school AIDS was not a problem, nobody knew about it. Teachers pointed out the methods of contraception and which were more effective and they said that the pill had a ninety-nine per cent success rate whereas the condom had a lot more risk involved. Now it's all changed.'

But has 'it all changed'? As the conversation went on, 'the pill' still emerged as the favoured method of contraception.

> *Norma*: If you sleep around, you'll have to take precautions (like the condom). If you have a serious relationship you'll have to think about it again.

Mandy suggests that the condom does not go with true love. 'If you love each other you wouldn't want to take precautions of that type (the condom).'

As the conversation progressed the pill was clearly favoured over the condom.

> *Norma*: The pill is such an easy method of contraception.
> *Mandy*: It's easier for girls to go to the family planning clinic than for boys to go to the chemist. It's over and done with.
> *Norma*: I think people should not have sex until they are sure and then stick to the pill. You don't need condoms.

Lara pointed out that young men might find it difficult to face their responsibilities clearly and use condoms. 'I think boys are going to have more problems coping with it 'cos girls have to use contraception or they're going to get pregnant so they are already cautious towards sex. Before, boys could just go around for years trying to push the responsibility for contraception onto girls. Now everybody is trying to push it back onto them. I don't know how they will respond to it.'

Sharon asserted that condoms were not safe anyway. ''The condom is not a safe method of contraception on its own anyway. If people were dependent on the condom just because it protects you from all these diseases a lot of people will get pregnant anyway. It's not a safe method.'

This continuing willingness to take 'the pill' is quite surprising. Clearly the fear of pregnancy continues to be a major concern for some of these young women. They have not yet fully assimilated the idea that sexually transmitted diseases might be an even greater hazard than pregnancy itself.

Before you rape me will you use a condom?

Two weeks before these discussion groups on AIDS had taken place the school had invited the women from 'Rape Crisis' to talk to sixth formers. The women who came were workers from the local 'Rape Crisis' centre. Their task is to keep the telephone line open for emergency calls and counsel and support rape victims.

The girls in this discussion group had very strong opinions about the presentation by 'Rape Crisis'. The issues were prominent in their thoughts and inevitably spilled over into the discussion about AIDS. Their criticism was that during the discussions on rape the presenters viewed all men as potential rapists. They all felt that this exaggerated the problem.

Abigail: The majority of men wouldn't think of raping women.
Sharon: I don't think we should look on men as a threat.

However, as the discussion continued it was clear that many of the girls were very afraid of assault and rape and felt this to be a constant menace.

Sharon: I think I am more afraid of getting attacked on the street than catching AIDS. That's one thing at the top of my list. I'm really worried about getting murdered, grabbed, tied up, bundled into a car, sexually assaulted. I don't know if it's because there is so much publicity about it.

Many of the girls were afraid to go out alone at night.

Lara: Yes I'd put being attacked above AIDS at my time of life. I wouldn't go out at night when it's dark, not any distance at night.
Marilyn: I'm even afraid going home from school through the underpass.

Rape has become even more dangerous now with the possibility of catching AIDS and other sexually transmitted diseases.

Marilyn: Rape is a terrible thing anyway.
Kate: More terrible now.
Debbie: But there's nothing you can do about it is there? You can't really say, 'Before you rape me will you use a condom? I've got one in my bag.'

Everybody laughed at this and yet the fear of assault and rape obviously controlled their sense of freedom out in the world.

Rape Crisis centres provide support for rape victims and initiate vital debates about the crime of rape. But because Rape Crisis highlights the relationship between sexuality and violence there was reluctance on the part of these young women to accept all of the presentation.

On one level they are very aware that they can easily become victims of male aggression and sexual violence, but this is not the sum total of their relationships with men. In the session with 'Rape crisis' there was no acknowledgement that most of the young women present *wanted* to establish sexual relations with young men. Therefore they found the conflict between the facts of assault and rape difficult to assimilate given their own sexual awareness and desires.

Conclusion

These girls are quite well informed about AIDS. They are not all well informed about other sexually transmitted diseases. The inadequate levels of knowledge mean that these young women are unable to appreciate their own vulnerability. They accept that casual heterosexual sex has become quite dangerous but because they believe that their chances of catching the HIV virus are not great they also reject the idea of using condoms. They do not realize that condoms give protection against many other sexually transmitted diseases (apart from the HIV virus), some of which have also reached epidemic proportions.

The suggestion by these girls that mutual trust in a relationship is a safeguard against the HIV virus or any other sexually transmitted disease may lead them to take unnecessary chances one of which is to take the birth-control pill. Most of the girls in the discussion still consider the birth-control pill to be the best method of contraception despite publicity about its side effects. It facilitates the other agenda of these conversations which is the establishment of heterosexual relationships. The pill may be a 'safe' method of contraception in the limited sense of preventing pregnancy but it is certainly not a protector of women's health. Reliance on 'the pill' is already a reliance on the integrity of your sexual partner. There are always going to be cases where this trust is not justified, for a number of reasons. First, potential sexual partners may be unaware of their exposure to a sexually transmitted disease. Second, checking on sexual histories is very difficult. It is an area where there may be strategic lapses of memory however good the intentions. It is now becoming clear that when you have sex with one person you have sex with everybody in their sexual past. Third, checking a potential partner's sexual history could become impossibly complex. In our society many relationships, however serious, do not last. The problem is not one which can be solved permanently but may continue through life with increasing complexity.

The girls were aware of some of these issues but in the end needed ways of coping with the risks associated with sex which still allowed them to establish sexual relationships.

As Lynda Measor suggests in Chapter 4, sex education has to negotiate with the meanings and experiences of sexuality which young people themselves reveal or it runs the risk of being ignored. Knowledge of the facts is very important in making an informed choice as long as the facts can be given in environments which inform rather than terrify, and which enable wider discussions about sexuality.

To approach these issues outside of more general discussions about sexuality may not be successful. However well presented, if the facts do not allow a consideration of sexual needs and desires they may well be dismissed.

Appendix

Clinics

There are 230 special clinics for sexually transmitted diseases and their reports show that since the 1950s new cases of STDs have increased from 100,000 to 600,000 in 1984. Dr R. S. Morton suggests that the nature of the problem has changed in one major respect. 'In the past 30 years the overall ratio of men to women patients has changed from 3:1 to 1:2 in 1984.' This is because, apart from AIDS, women are very susceptible to catching STDs such as genital warts and genital herpes and complications are often more severe.

Syphilis

Syphilis is not really a public health problem. The number of cases in 1984 was only 3307 (Morton 1987).

Gonorrhoea

The incidence of gonorrhoea has been dropping in the last ten years. There were 54,000 cases in 1984 (Morton 1987).

Non-specific genital infection (NSGI)

There were 155,000 cases reported by Special Clinics in 1984. Chlamydia trachomatis has been shown to be a major causative organism. It is undoubtedly the most common sexually transmitted cause of urethritis (Worm and Petersen 1987, pp. 19-21). The relationship between NSGI and pelvic inflammatory disease in women remains unclear. However Worm and Petersen suggest that the use of the condom is the most effective means of ensuring that these infections are not transmitted.

Genital herpes

The figures for the number of cases of genital herpes are difficult to ascertain as sufferers may return to special clinics with repeat attacks. However, the number of cases reported by STD clinics has trebled from 1975 to 1984 to about 20,000. Morton (1987) reports that the increase in women was six times that in men and points out that there is a correlation between genital herpes and cancer of the cervix. There may be danger to a baby during birth if the mother has an attack during labour. It can be fatal to the newborn child.

Genital warts

This is a widespread problem. Genital warts have reached epidemic proportion in some areas. The STD clinics report 50,000 cases in 1984 but this is undoubtedly not the total of all sufferers. There is now considerable evidence of an association between wart virus infections of the cervix and pre-malignant changes in cervical cells.

A study by the British Co-operative Clinical Group drew attention to the high proportion of abnormalities in cervical smears from the under-25 age group attending STD clinics during their three-month study of 116 clinics. They suggest that information from teaching hospitals indicates that past or present genital warts were associated with these cytological abnormalities of the cervix in young women (BCCG 1987, pp. 40-3). Unfortunately women under

25 are probably less likely to concern themselves with regular smear tests, even if the facilities were available.

Cervical cancer

This is now Britain's commonest life-threatening form of sexually transmitted disease. Every year 2000 women die from cervical cancer and yet it is preventable in many cases if early diagnosis had taken place.

There is now evidence that sexual transmission is an aspect of cervical cancer. In a recent edition of the *British Medical Journal* a GP wrote to enquire about risks of cancer to a young woman who lived with a man whose previous wife had died of cervical cancer.

In reply an obstetrician and gynaecologist J. O. Drife made it clear that a woman's own sexual history and health records were important but the role of a male partner was very relevant.

> If this patient's husband has a job that means frequent absence from home she has a higher chance of developing cancer of the cervix presumably because such a job increases the chance of extra-marital coitus. Her risk is related to the number of her husband's partners and is particularly high if he has recourse to prostitutes. (Drife 1986)

The response goes on to discuss a study in the USA of women married to men whose previous wives had cervical cancer. So far there have been 2.7 times the expected number of cervical cancers.

AIDS

By the end of 1986 over 600 cases of AIDS had been diagnosed of whom half had died. These figures are estimated to double approximately every ten months. It is also estimated that about 30,000 people are incubating the HIV virus.

The government has spent £2.6 million on a campaign to raise public awareness of the dangers of casual sex because of AIDS and the need for barrier contraceptive protection especially the use of the condom.

Cervical smear tests

It is vital to women's health to have access to cervical smear tests for the sexually active female population, and an explanation of cervical smear tests and an emphasis on the need for regular smears should be part of all sex education classes for girls. Unfortunately facilities for testing continue to be inadequate. Still we must not give up teaching our young women to demand the facilities necessary to monitor their health.

Bibliography

British Co-operative Clinical Group (1987) *Genitourinary Medicine*, Vol. 63, pp. 40–3.

Department of Education and Science (1987) *AIDS: Some Questions and Answers*. Facts for Teachers, Lecturers and Youth Workers.

Drife, James Owen's reply to a letter in *British Medical Journal*, Vol. 292, 11 January 1986.

Morton, R. S. (1987) 'Control of Sexually Transmitted Diseases Today and Tomorrow', *Genitourinary Medicine*, Vol. 63, pp. 202–9.

Worm, A. and Petersen, C. S. (1987) 'Transmission of Chlamydial Infections to Sexual Partners', *Genitourinary Medicine*, Vol. 63, pp. 19–21.

CHAPTER 4

'Are you coming to see some dirty films today?' Sex Education and Adolescent Sexuality

LYNDA MEASOR

This chapter looks at patterns of adolescent sexuality as they are observable in a school context, and at the character of school-based sex education lessons. The data is taken from a research project in a large, urban, East Midlands comprehensive where I spent eighteen months doing participant observation, interviewing a group of pupils aged twelve and over. The chapter focuses upon the quality and character of sex education in schools, and specifically on pupils' reactions to it.

When I looked in detail at the way one school handles sex education lessons, a number of points emerged. The teachers who undertook sex education lessons were well meaning, they were specifically trained for the job and they put an enormous amount of planning and thought into the lessons. Nevertheless, I want to claim that the gap between the lessons and the adolescent's sexual world is enormous, and I shall document that with reference to the research data. These teachers failed to address many of the issues most central to the pupils' concerns. Instead the sex education they provided was derived from their own culture, and from their adult status. The history of the content of sex education in lessons undoubtedly has its roots in the radical ideas of women like Marie Stopes early in this century. It is not surprising therefore that sex education is not child centred, or, more accurately, adolescent centred. It is not informed by, nor does it take its cues from, the world of adolescent sexuality.

Sex education lessons

My starting point is the reaction of the group of twelve-year-old
pupils to their sex education lessons, which took place in this study
in the summer term of their first year at secondary school. The
majority of pupils appeared very embarrassed, although this
resulted in a range of different reactions. The pupils were shown a
number of films on human reproduction and birth. They then had a
number of follow-up lessons to discuss the issues raised in the films,
and to allow them to ask questions of their teachers. A typical scene
was as follows.

> *Teacher*: The pupils get me after registration, we all walk over to the
> lecture theatre. There is an air of excitement and a feel that this is
> not any old Wednesday morning in the air.

Two boys talk to me.

> *Keith*: Hey miss, are you coming to see some rude films
> with us?
> *Pete*: Are you coming to see some dirty films today?

The group is joined by another two forms of pupils; all file into the
lecture theatre. The teacher explains that they will today see a film
on human reproduction and birth. As he talks, several of the girls
blush furiously, and seem very embarrassed. The film begins. One
girl sits for the whole film hiding her face, with her hands across her
eyes. There are again a lot of signals of embarrassment, boys nudge
each other and giggle, the atmosphere is rather uncomfortable.

After the film, the pupils all spent a lot of time discussing it, and
their feelings and reactions to it. Many of the girls said they felt
embarrassed, confirming the impression they had given in the lecture theatre.

> *Rebecca*: I was embarrassed, watching the film; you are all together
> as a class and that, so frightened to make a move.
> *Roz*: She really went bright red [said to Rebecca]. And Claire couldn't
> watch.
> *Jenny*: You do get embarrassed.

The embarrassment is not very surprising, but some of the girls had
a sense that it was not really 'proper' to be discussing matters sexual
in school.

> *Amy*: Well me mum's already told me all about it anyway.

Amy suggests here that home and family and conversations with her mum count as the 'proper' territory for matters emotional.

Debbie made this clearer: 'My mum told me about periods, when she used to wash me, in the bath. I had long hair, it got really tangled, and my mum used to do it, and wash it out for me, and she used to tell me all about it in the bathroom.'

For Debbie, it was at such moments of shared mother–daughter intimacy that sexual information should be exchanged.

Sally had a similar account: 'I just went into my mum's room first of all, and she goes, "What have you come to see me about?" and I goes, "Nothing," and then she just told me. She just got this little book out about marriage and things like that.'

Jenny also talked to her mum and she contrasted this sharply with her experience at school: 'Like Sally, my mum told me about periods and that, when I was in the bath, but in my old school we did a film on seeing babies born and I remember looking at it and not thinking at all . . . not really understanding.'

Clearly it is mothers who undertake these responsibilities for emotional education with the girls.

The girls also specifically objected to sharing their sex education lessons with the boys. A group of boys discussed the film they had seen with me.

Keith: Was you in our interesting science lesson then?
Phillip: Yes, we're having a film about a girl becoming a woman.
Dominic: Yes . . . about menstruation . . . whatever this is . . .

Janet listened to this exchange and then commented quietly to me, 'It is really embarrassing doing all those films with the boys there.'

Jenny agreed, 'It's awful.'

Sally chimed in, 'I hate it with the boys there, when they're talking about periods and things like that.'

When I interviewed the girls in more depth, the same kind of reaction was clear.

Amy: The boys just laugh and things. It's all right for them.
Claire: You do get embarrassed, because all the boys sit there going Corr! Look at that!
Interviewer: Would it be less embarrassing if the boys weren't there?
Both: Yes, really.

There has been a considerable amount of debate recently on the idea of placing girls in single-sex groups for particular parts of the curriculum. Perhaps sex education should be included in this debate.

The girls also said they found it difficult to cope when sex education was given by a male teacher.

> *Amy*: You want to ask questions, but we have a male science teacher and you can't.
>
> *Debbie*: With a male science teacher, you think twice about asking a question.

In this school, since there were no female science teachers, all the sex education lessons were done by men.

The girls also resented the fact that both the film and the discussion afterwards had concentrated too much on girls, and on girls' bodies, and on the female role in reproduction. Their objections were fair. There were far more pictures of naked female bodies in the films than of male.

Jenny made this point. 'Well our teacher, in those classes, always talked about girls, girls this, periods, bodies, girls that, and he never said a thing about boys, so I asked what a wet dream was. I know what one was, but I wanted him to actually say it, so all the boys could be embarrassed, like we had been. But he only said about seven words, and I was really annoyed. Why can't he speak about boys?'

Sally had perceived things in the same way. 'It annoyed me, because when we talked about girls and periods, we had a whole film on it . . . but when it came to the boys, we didn't really know anything. The boys knew every single fact about girls, but we never knew a thing about boys which I don't think is right, because if they can learn about us, we ought to learn about them.'

These then were the girls' stated objections to sex education, and it is important to record their extreme discomfort, their embarrassment and their sense of being engaged in an activity that they did not feel was quite right. As adults we would not tolerate being placed in such a position. I want to question whether it is right to simply oppose their reactions and teach sex education regardless. At the very least we should be more aware of their objections, and aware of the reasons behind them, and attempt to sensitize sex education practitioners to the needs of adolescents.

Sex education in this school took a fresh, hearty, open-air approach to human sexuality, the human body and reproduction. However, from observation of the pupils, it seemed that the world of adolescent sexuality was rather different. For them the sexual world was covert, and mysterious; the way into it was not seen as open. Like other areas of adolescent culture, a way had to be won through to it. Its rules had to be discovered and negotiated.

Adolescent sexuality

A number of background points need to be made. When pupils first entered the school, there were some mixed-gender groupings in the classroom, depending on the organization of the lesson. If pupils were working around long tables, for example in art and craft subjects, then there were both boys and girls at the same table. Alternatively, when pupils sat in long rows of separate desks there were both boys and girls in the same row. Within six weeks of attending secondary school, the gender separation had become complete for these pupils. They always sat at separate tables and on separate sides of the room. When questioned, teachers made it clear that they were not responsible for the changes, and had certainly not asked for them.

The reasons for this sudden rigid separation have to be sought within developing adolescent sexuality. During the ages ten to twelve children withdraw at some point from cross-gender contact of a childhood kind. They thus signal that things are changing dramatically. When contact is resumed it will be of a different kind. Changing schools seemed to stand as a kind of external prop, which set off the other reactions. Limitations are placed on what boys and girls can and cannot do and for a while strong lines are drawn physically between them.

One of their problems and preoccupations is undoubtedly information. Pupils did want basic information about human sexuality and reproduction. Girls would spend a lot of time in small huddles discussing these matters. One rule of adolescent culture is that you must always pretend to know everything; you cannot admit to ignorance about any sexual matter. In the little groups of girls who sat around at lunchtime, there was status to be won or lost in the possession of knowledge about sexual matters. Amy and Claire described their own reactions if they did not know or understand something in such a discussion.

> *Amy*: I would pretend I knew.
> *Claire*: If we were in a group of girls and they said a word and I didn't know what it meant, I would pretend I knew.

Interviewer: Do you think you get teased if . . . [but before I had time
   to finish the question Amy interrupted].
Amy: She doesn't know, she is stupid.

On another occasion Sally and Jenny were discussing Caesarean section operations and the way they were done. A friend's mother had
just had such an operation. It illustrates how this kind of knowledge is
passed around and gained, and is dependent on friendship networks.
There was evidence that some pupils had wrong information.

Claire: My friend, she is about eight now, and she still doesn't know
   how to have a baby and that; she always thinks that you have got to
   go the hospital, have a pill and that will grow inside you, that is what
   she thinks.

Sometimes it was mothers who were said to be responsible for giving
the wrong information.

Amy: My mum told me not to take cold drinks like Coca-Cola, and she
   says that if you take Coca-Cola and fizzy drinks your period stops.

One area of adolescent anxiety relates to the different rates at which
young people mature. The girls discussed this a great deal. It is one of
the reasons behind their reluctance to take showers as a group.

Pat: I don't like the showers. On the first day we were ever so shy.
   Everyone has got things different . . . some people have got hairs
   some haven't.
Carole: There is one girl in our group . . . she is big chested and that,
   and she walks through the shower all covered up. It's best to be in
   between. We all giggle and throw our towels down. She finally went
   in the shower with her towel. There is one really little girl who sits
   there making faces, she looks at everyone, she makes you feel
   embarrassed.

The fact that some girls reached puberty and began their periods a
long time before others was also a source of anxiety and problems.

Roz: Two of my friends started (their periods) when they were ten, at
   middle school, and some of the boys knew, and made fun of them.
Amy: That's why being the last to start though – just about everyone
   has except me – you start thinking, 'What's wrong with me?' I think
   starting your periods makes you feel like a woman and grown up and
   that. Jackie and Janie, I don't think they have had theirs, because
   they act quite babyish don't they?

One simple recommendation to sex education teachers is that they
could include more material which deals specifically with the variable

in times of reaching puberty. Reassurance that different rates of maturing are normal and to be expected could be given.

The girls said that one of the problems with the sex education film they were shown was the naked women that were in it. It might be possible to question whether they were necessary to the message they were intending to give. There were other examples, apart from sex education lessons, where pupils' discomfort with nakedness was made clear, such as the comments girls made about taking showers as a group. On one occasion the art room had some life drawings pinned on the walls. They caused a lot of comment, especially from the boys. Roy said, 'Sir, who done that rude picture of that woman up there without a bra?' Again it was the naked female form that was up on the walls.

Despite their need for sexual information, these pupils found it difficult to discuss sexuality with adults and with their teachers. They also found it difficult to admit any ignorance publicly. Their teacher showed an awareness of these inhibitions. He organized a follow-up discussion lesson on the film and asked if there were any questions. He offered pupils the opportunity to write down their questions on folded paper and hand them in.

Learning sexual signalling

Besides the sex education lessons a less official task is learning the tactics of sexual signalling. Certainly this group of pupils spent an enormous amount of time working out how to do the signalling, and assessing whether they had got it right. In establishing 'who fancies who', pupils need to find out if they are the sort of person who is going to be successful in these adolescent sexual encounters. The risks are high, especially at first, when you have never tested your own appeal. Pupils need methods and tactics that signal their feelings and their attractions, but which keep the risks of rejection to an absolute minimum.

With this group the tactics grew in sophistication and confidence throughout the first year in the school, but at first appeared in a discreet and covert form. Once pupils had withdrawn into their single-sex groups, experimentation began. The girls did a lot of passive watching and signalling at first, as they dreamed over boys they felt attracted to. Roz sat watching Bruce out of the chemistry lab window. 'Oh I think he's lovely, I really fancy him,' she would repeat in soft sentimental tones. They also spent a lot of time discussing rock stars and poring over the pictures of them and football stars that they brought into school.

Particular individuals were braver than others however, and risks began to be taken. The first method tried was 'writing on pencil cases'. Aprons and 'rough books' were then fairly rapidly employed. Girls would write the name of a boy on a particular girl's pencil case. Amy, for example, went to fetch a piece of equipment. When she returned she noticed a new piece of graffiti and she was annoyed: 'Oohh! who's written Amy likes Andrew on my pencil case? – It's not true . . . I don't like him.' Sally laughed and said, 'No, it's Gary isn't it?' This Amy did not deny. From such beginnings likings could be made more public. Girls gained the confidence to write boys' names on their own pencil cases or rulers. This may help explain why boys and girls continued to sit apart in the classroom, and why furious fights broke out when boys tried to borrow equipment like rulers and projectors from girls. Such action broke the covert nature of the liking. Girls did not yet openly want the boys to know who 'fancied who'.

New tactics emerged slowly, appropriate to the girls' emerging needs. Girls would also write 'I love   ' with a blank space for the name, on the front of their hands. This signalled their general interest in cross-gender involvements; it did not risk any rejection. On the palm of their hands they would write the name; the palm could be more easily hidden, was less on public show. The style of these tactics was to allow enough information to filter through to the boy involved, so that he could act if he chose, but equally to allow the girl to retreat without embarrassment. Girls can communicate in a range of other ways with the object of their fancy – for example they can stare at him, walk close to him, comb their hair and giggle when he enters the room – while very little is being committed to public knowledge.

Amy and Jenny wrote the names of particular boys on each other's craft aprons. The activity involves a good deal of giggling excitement. Amy would not write 'Amy loves Martin' on her own apron, but was prepared to allow Jenny to write it on hers. She can always make a public disclaimer and say, 'Oh Jenny wrote that'. She also insisted that Jenny must keep the apron secreted away. 'Don't go around wearing that will you.' Nevertheless, Amy was taking a more public risk than was usual, she was negotiating new territory. Later on, as confidence grew more, likings were made yet more public, but pupils still covered themselves. Individual pupils took it upon themselves to acquaint others with the facts. Amy, for example, said to Pete, 'Everyone knows you fancy Roz. She does you an' all.' At a school disco Sally asked Roy to dance with Jenny.

Risks were taken for girls on behalf of their friends. It avoided a face-to-face rejection. In addition, the girl involved could always vociferously deny that she had anything to do with the communication. Jenny, for example, protested, 'I didn't know anything about it. Sally just went off and up to Roy. I never asked her to do it.' A certain amount of protection was offered. Amy and Claire discussed just how scary the whole thing was.

> *Amy*: You have got to be careful what you say. I don't want to look an idiot.
> *Claire*: It is terrible if you like someone. You want to tell them.
> *Amy*: How much you care.
> *Claire*: And you want to tell them but you can't.
> *Amy*: Some boy really fancies you, and you really fancy them but you can't put it together.
> *Claire*: You can't say 'I like you'.

This again helps to explain why girls do not sit next to boys in class.

> *Claire*: I always sit with a girl. I never sit with a boy.
> *Amy*: I have to sit next to a boy in English, I have no choice.
> *Claire*: They all take the mickey and say, 'Oh look, that's a new girlfriend'.

Sitting next to someone is a way of 'telling them you really like them', of making a bond; an action that would leave a pupil exposed and without cover.

The basic rule of the new approved sexual signalling was ambiguity, involving a series of covert messages which made the fact that 'Roz liked Pete' both clear and unclear at the same time. If a boy knows 'you like him', but does not reciprocate, the girl is in trouble, for major ridicule can result. This is a situation to avoid at all costs, and therefore a number of subterfuges and partial cover-ups need to be negotiated, allowing the girl to withdraw from the commitment if there are no reciprocated feelings and to pretend that she was not really interested at all.

The following example reveals very clearly the sanctions and penalties that could result if a girl failed to negotiate effectively.

> *Christine*: There's a boy in our class I like at the moment. He's nice

he is . . . I didn't want anyone to tell 'im. I wanted it to be a secret.

Amina: Someone wrote a letter to him and signed it for Christine, and he called her names.

Jacqui: It was somebody in our class. Every girl in our class knew who it was Christine liked and that letter was made by stencil so you couldn't tell who wrote it. He really called her horrible names, and wrote a note with horrible things in it and gave it to Christine.

Everyone in Christine's class knew about the situation, and many of the girls laughed at her. Matthew himself was furious and constantly referred to Christine as a 'stupid bag' and systematically ignored her when he was not being insulting.

The double standard

This raises a further issue. It rapidly became clear that the double standard for sexual conduct was alive and well in this school. The data from this research supports Paul Willis (1978) in indicating that two kinds of girls are perceived by the boys. One is the kind you have as a girlfriend, the other is a 'tart'. The girls in this study were very aware of that distinction, and they accepted it, and they went to enormous lengths to avoid ever 'getting a reputation'. They made no challenge to the notion of the double standard; it was an accepted part of their lives. The girls identified a number of prohibitions. If these were transgressed, then sanctions would result, and the dreaded name of 'tart' would be applied to the offender. The prohibition concerned appearance and make-up, clothes, language and of course sexual conduct. In this paper it is only possible to summarize the data.

Amy: They said that if you get too much for yourself, they'll have you.

Interviewer: What does getting too much for yourself mean?

Amy: My sister said if you try to act old and try to be in fashion with everybody in the older year, they are just going to go against you. First at school I tried to wear something that was really old, because I tried something on and my sister said, 'Don't wear that, you know, they'll all be making fun of you.' So I took that off and went in something horrible.

Make-up was another item of major importance on the prohibited list.

> *Vivien*: Sometimes I wear eye shadow, but lipstick and that looks horrible.

Jacqui was in agreement.

> *Jacqui*: I only wear eye shadow. I wouldn't wear blusher stuff and that.
> *Kerry*: You get a reputation – 'She wears make-up. Look at her' – and all that. It is like this girl in this school, she wears great black eye shadow and blusher.
> *Jacqui*: Yes they call her horrible names, like tart, and say she's easy to get and things like that, 'Look at that slut, look at her waiting on the corner again.'

Specific clothes have particularly heavy symbolic weight in this code.

> *Jenny*: You get those names though. I am scared to wear my pencil skirt. I have a navy blue one. It is nice, but I don't wear it at school really, because of getting called names.

There were a number of girls who had transgressed this code, and who had got reputations. The description of Sylvia and Donna repeated some of the issues.

> *Sally*: Sylvia, well I hope you don't mind me saying so, she's a bit of a tart as well.
> *Interviewer*: Is she? Why?
> *Sally*: Well she comes to school in that pencil skirt. She wears nothing but that stupid pencil skirt.
> *Jenny*: She wears ever such low tops.
> *Sally*: Yes.
> *Jenny*: She wears spotted tights with great big high heels to school.
> *Sally*: And she wears quite a bit of make-up.

But the description revealed some of the other issues. They dealt with the conduct of cross-gender encounters.

> *Sally*: I don't know, she flirts around with the boys as well. She was going out with Pete. She was kissing him and everything, then she packed him in.
> *Jenny*: Her mum turned around and said she was going to take her to a psychiatrist.

The same accusation was made against Roz, although the degree of severity was much less.

Amy: At the disco she was flirting around with Pete, and she got off with him, as if she was going out with him, but she wasn't properly and the boys think, 'Oh, she will go with anybody.'

These girls fail to learn the sexual signalling language properly; they 'make it obvious' that they are interested in boys, and they break the covert code.

Amy: Roz is called 'tart' and everything like that.
Claire: You see her brushing her hair, putting lip gloss on, doing this, and make-up on, and always looking at herself.
Amy: Thinking that all the boys will turn around.
Claire: She can get you a bad name if you're not careful.
Amy: I don't want a bad name as I go through school.
Claire: Yes she flirts with any boys she sees.

The sanctions were not imaginary in the girls' minds; they met a fair amount of harassment and abuse from the boys if any transgression occurred. They could also meet abuse from older girls in the school. Such pressures had an enormous effect on the girls. Amina made a general complaint about the lower status of girls.

Amina: The boys can be rude.
Jane: They don't even like talking to girls really.

There were other specific accounts of sexual harassment.

Jenny: You have to do PE in the hall in shorts and everything, all up on the climbing frame.
Interviewer: Don't you like doing PE in your shorts?
Jenny: Yes, but the boys sort of take the mickey out of you.
Interviewer: Do they?
Jenny: They all come up and start whistling and everything. Yes, and they all come round and look in the windows and knock on them.
Sally: You expect boys to be a bit crude about things like that.

Girls met some teasing about their appearance and sexual development, or lack of it: 'When I wear a pencil skirt, my brothers say, "You look like a pencil." They say things like, "If you had a red head, you'd be a match." And yes, "If you go on strike you will flare up." '

If a girl once got a 'reputation' then the sanctions could become stronger.

Roz: The boys have been calling us prostitutes and tarts recently.
Amy: Where's your red lights? and that.
Roz: Because of these red socks.
Interviewer: Who have they said that to?

Amy: Roz.

Roz: We told Mrs Cornfield and she goes, 'Tell them they are silly boys.' I think she should do more about them calling us tarts and prostitutes. It isn't nice because we're not.

The sanctions applied to Sylvia got progressively stronger as the year went on.

Jacqui: Someone wrote on the desk, 'What do you think of Sylvia Dutch?' and there were all these names underneath.

Janie: Saying she acts like a tart or something.

Jacqui: Yes, everyone calls her that.

Janie: Some people call Christine that and she gets annoyed.

Jacqui: No, they are only mucking about with her, but you can tell they are not mucking about with Donna.

Donna was the other example of a girl who completely transgressed the limits. Within three days of entering the school she had sworn roundly at her teacher. Her first year in the school was marked by repeated suspensions; she was constantly in serious trouble. She was reviled by the other girls for 'having a loud mouth'. She was known universally as a tart. It was alleged that she became pregnant and had an abortion in the course of her first year in the school. She became the victim of actual sexual harassment and abuse, once this reputation was fully established. At a local disco, a group of boys surrounded her, and removed virtually all of her clothes. This was widely discussed and known about. At the end of the summer term a group of boys from the school took her to a lonely part of the school grounds after school hours and subjected her to a range of sexual abuse. It was stopped from going any further by the surprise arrival of a teacher.

Interviewer: If a boy went out with loads of girls would you think the same about him?

Jenny: No, they don't, do they?

Girls then are not supposed to be openly interested in sex in this adolescent culture, at least in this age grade in a provincial town. They are not supposed to dress provocatively, their appearance and faces have to be modest. They are not allowed to openly take the initiative in approaching a boy, they have to learn covert signals. They can face sexual harassment if they fail to learn the code (see also Lees 1986). The sex education the girls received took no account of any of these pressures within their culture; and in fact confronted them directly. It is important to question whether a direct confrontation is

the best way to deal with and help pupils to cope with the pressures
they experience. Again single-sex groups for the subject would help.

By its 'open air heartiness', sex education in this school conflicted
with the realities of adolescent sexual culture. I want to suggest that
as a result it was difficult for the sex educators to reach or meet the
needs of the adolescents. The sex education remained a distant,
unhelpful, adult thing as a result. It seems important to recognize
these realities, and to look for methods which allow sex education
practitioners to get closer to the adolescents' world, and to violate
their culture a little less. The need is for a middle ground, a range of
tactics to bridge the gap between adult and adolescents' worlds, so
that both sides can meet in the middle. Single-sex groupings might
be a starting point, for example. Another is to choose films and
other teaching materials which avoid such open display of the naked
female body.

Bibliography

Lees S. (1986) *Losing out: How girls become wives*, Hutchinson.
Willis, P. (1978) *Learning to Labour*, Saxon House.

CHAPTER 5

Child Sexual Abuse and the Role of the Teacher

JENNY KITZINGER

The sexual abuse of children has recently been 'discovered' as a major social problem and abused children are now being encouraged to seek help by widespread publicity, such as Childwatch. This kind of publicity has led to more and more children taking the risk of confiding in a trusted adult and there has been a rapid increase in the number of cases referred to Social Services and the NSPCC. One-third of all reports of abuse come via the school. Teachers are often among the few adults outside the family network with whom children have regular contact, so when abused children feel unable to tell anyone at home (perhaps because the abuser lives with them or is considered a friend of the family), they often turn to them for help. Teachers are also in a good position to notice changes in a child's behaviour, and to respond when a child seems hurt or depressed. They are in a key position in the struggle to help sexually abused children and many are taking on this challenge by introducing anti-sexual-abuse programmes into the classrooms and demanding training to develop their skills in detecting and responding to abused children.

Over the last few years I have worked with young women needing to leave home because of sexual abuse. Often these young women originally told someone at school about the abuse and sometimes it was because of a teacher's support, or publicity material made available at school, that they were able to find help. I have also been writing a book about sexual abuse based on interviews with adult survivors. Many of the women I have interviewed never told anyone about the abuse at the time. Others did try to tell a teacher but were met with incomprehension or disbelief. Sadly, the pain and disillusionment these women describe is still familiar to some children seeking help today. The stories these women tell can help us to consider what kind of policies and practices we should be introducing into schools to support children who are being abused now.

In this chapter I draw on the words of survivors of child sexual abuse to explore the role that can be played by the teacher.[1] I also draw on discussions with teachers themselves, particularly those who have attended training workshops that I have run on this subject. From these workshops I have realized just how threatening and anxiety-provoking the whole issue of child sexual abuse is – especially for teachers, who often find themselves in a double-bind and feel trapped whatever they do. I have also seen how committed many teachers are to tackling this difficult issue and making themselves available to children who need help.

Nobody finds child sexual abuse an easy subject to discuss. It can make us feel disgusted, angry, sad, hurt and embarrassed. Some people try to protect themselves by evading the issue or preferring to believe that child sexual abuse doesn't really happen very often. Other people distance themselves from the problem by stating that child sexual abuse only happens in other communities or cultures – not their own. The sexual abuse of children is a subject surrounded by barriers of prejudice, misinformation and sensationalism. A good basic discussion of some of the myths that surround, and obscure, child sexual abuse, and specifically incest, is Sarah Nelson's short book *Incest: Fact and myth*. This is a book well worth reading, discussing with colleagues and then keeping in the school library.

Once teachers have overcome the barriers of disbelief and seen through the myths that obscure child sexual abuse, they still face very specific questions about how to react to the possibility that one of their pupils is being abused: 'How can I tell?' 'How should I react if a child confides in me?' 'What happens then?' In this chapter I will try to suggest answers to all these questions and point to ways in which teachers can try to help children to avoid sexual assault.

How can I tell if a child is being sexually abused?

One of the first questions teachers ask is: 'I know about black eyes as a sign of *physical* abuse, but what are the signs of sexual abuse?'

Although sexual abuse can sometimes result in physical signs, such as bruises on the thighs or 'love bites', teachers will usually have to rely on the child's behavioural and verbal cues. Teachers constantly draw on their experience of working with children to respond to those who are unhappy or disturbed whatever the cause. There are, however, specific signs related to sexual abuse. Check-lists, like the one below, appear on leaflets available for teachers (see resource list):

Signs that may be displayed by a sexually abused child

1 Aggression, disruptive and attention-seeking behaviour or, alternatively, overly compliant behaviour
2 Sexually explicit writing/drawing or so-called 'provocative' behaviour or displays of sexual knowledge inappropriate to the child's age
3 Acute shame and apparent distaste for own body
4 Isolation, having few school friends
5 Eating disorders
6 Depression, anxiety, being withdrawn, fearful, or clingy and dependent
7 Secretiveness/lying/day-dreaming or fantasizing 'excessively'
8 Poor school performance or sudden fall in school performance
9 Truanting or, alternatively, reluctance to go home and running away from home
10 Tummy pains without medical cause, constant tiredness, incontinence
11 Being 'accident-prone', self-injury or suicide attempts.

Such check-lists are a useful reference point but they are not fail-proof. They can, for instance, be criticized for giving the impression that there is one, unproblematic, 'normal' standard of behaviour that can be applied to all children, whereas, of course, children's behaviour will vary depending on their own cultural and family background. There are many problems with definition. For example, what counts as 'sexual knowledge inappropriate to the child's age'? Such check-lists can also not be relied on to alert us to the child who behaves very 'normally' at school, and many children are careful to show no overt signs of abuse at all. Teachers are also critical of such lists because they feel that the type of behaviour listed is often displayed by non-abused children:

> If this list had been around in my day I'm sure they'd have packed me off for an anal examination – I was always hurting myself but *I* wasn't sexually abused!
>
> But most admission kids behave in many of these ways when they first come to a new school – at least half my class fit the description!

These statements, in part, reflect the teachers' own anxieties – check-lists, like the one listed above, are meant as guide-lines; it was never intended that they be used as absolute diagnostic tools. They are of limited value if used in isolation without some understanding of how they were derived. If teachers are to make appropriate use of such check-lists it is helpful to see each type of behaviour in context, to explore what it means to the child, and *why* a combination of such behaviour may be associated with sexual abuse. One way of looking at the behaviour of sexually abused children is to see it in terms of coping skills – the skills that children develop to help them survive abuse. Some behaviour represents ways in which a child may try to protect herself from abuse (e.g. by avoiding the abuser, or trying not to think about it). Other types of behaviour may be a child's way of asking for help or, alternatively, her way of trying to prevent anyone from discovering the abuse. (Children will often try to tell someone about the abuse while at the same time trying to hide it because they want to share the terrible secret and get help but at the same time fear the consequences.) The behaviour of an abused child may also be a direct reaction to the way the abuse makes her feel (e.g. sexual abuse can make a child feel dirty so she may appear very ashamed of her own body).

To understand how these different ways of coping with abuse operate it is useful to listen to survivors talking about what the abuse meant for them and how it affected their behaviour at school. For instance, the check-lists mention that abused children can appear very isolated at school. This is a theme that comes up again and again in the comments of adult survivors who recall feeling 'marked' or 'different':

> I knew somehow that I was different from other kids, I felt I was tainted, and that something was wrong with me forever. It was like invisible scars from a childhood disease.
>
> (quoted in Armstrong, 1987, p. 16)

A child who is being abused may feel alienated from her contemporaries. She is constantly wary, 'acting a part' to protect herself from exposure:

> How could I be friends and chat in the playground? They laugh and talk as if they know it all, but I do know it all and I have to be careful not to give anything away.
>
> (Lorraine, quoted in Maher, 1987, p. 129)

Self-injury and being 'accident-prone' is another 'symptom' of abuse commonly mentioned in check-lists – such injuries could, in fact, be caused by batterings from the abuser, they could be self-inflicted as a form of self-punishment (many abused children feel intensely guilty) or they could be a child's way of asking for help. Some abused children deliberately hurt themselves in the hope that someone will ask them what the matter is or simply give them some care and attention. Nita used to throw herself down a slope until her knees were torn and bleeding, trying to show how much she was hurting inside ('Breaking Silence' 1986). Other children incorporate hints about it in drawings or essays. One girl handed in an essay detailing the sexual abuse inflicted on her by their lodger. Her teacher was angry and wrote, 'I can't imagine what induced you to write about such a subject, no examiner would be impressed' (Childwatch 1985).

The acute shyness and self-consciousness listed as a sign of abuse also echoes the stories from adult survivors about their shame and their childhood attempts to hide the fact that they were being abused. Sexually abused children sometimes feel that their guilty secret is obvious to everyone – almost as if they were branded. Sally says she always felt people might be able to tell that she was 'having sex' with her uncle and was 'sexually experienced' just by looking at her. She would, therefore, never stand up in class or draw attention to herself in any way. She also avoided undressing in front of other people 'because I felt that they were all looking at me' and, she adds, 'I often had these bruises on my thighs.'

Sally also describes behaviour which matches another 'sign of abuse' in the check-lists – reluctance to go home as a young child and, later, running away as a teenager. She sees this as one way in which she tried to protect herself and avoid her father's sexual demands:

> At primary school the other children used to run home at three o'clock but I used to say to the teacher 'do you want anything doing?'.
> I wanted to stay, school was the only place I felt safe.

Some abused children do very well at school; they work hard and are seen as good pupils. Other children, however, find they are unable to concentrate in lessons or they respond to their own pain and confusion by becoming 'naughty' or 'bad'. They may make up stories, steal, bully, and may be labelled as 'sexually provocative' because they have been taught that their only worth is their sexual attractiveness. Often this alienates teachers and makes them less ready to believe any allegations of sexual abuse made by that child. It is ironic that the very behaviour that can be produced in a child because of sexual abuse can act against that child being believed should she try to tell anyone about the abuse. Teachers spend a lot of time trying to maintain discipline in over-crowded class-rooms, and a 'difficult' or 'attention-seeking' child is, at best, a nuisance. However, while such reactions from teachers are understandable, and perhaps an inevitable part of the current school system, it is important to remember that such behaviour may be the result of a child's struggle to cope with sexual abuse – sexually abused children are not 'problem children', they are children with problems.

Looking back, some adult survivors describe themselves as hateful and disruptive children hiding their vulnerability behind a façade of toughness. Tina, who was abused by her uncle, describes herself as a schoolgirl full of hate – hate for herself and hostility towards others:

> I wasn't too bad in the first year because he was only touching me up then, and the worst he'd ever do was push his hands up inside me. But in the second year it just got worse and I wasn't nice to be around, you didn't want to be with me . . . I was always fighting. I'd really hurt people. I knew I would. I'd never show any mercy of any kind, I was very ruthless. I was quite horrible. I didn't want to show anyone how weak I really was.

Tina ended up being sent to Borstal because of her violence. Teachers may question such disturbed behaviour, but, if the child is seen as a trouble-maker, they may demand explanations as justification rather than genuinely creating the space for the child to talk. Fiona, who was abused by her father from when she was four years old until her teens, was often in trouble at school. She wishes someone had been genuinely interested in why she behaved as she did but feels she was never given the chance to explain:

> I was very disturbed at that stage and got into an awful lot of trouble but nobody was asking the right questions. There were so many times, there were so many people who could have approached me and if they had had just a wee bit of insight.

On one occasion Fiona came close to telling a teacher who confronted her about her behaviour:

> I more or less started to say something but they said something and it was just so fiercesome . . . there is this pressure when someone is

getting at you for something, you want to tell them the whole story – 'you haven't got it quite right, I want to tell you something that might make you think slightly differently of me'. But they didn't give me a chance . . . There were a couple of times when people clearly questioned why I had a certain attitude, why I was behaving the way I did, and I knew the answer but I wasn't free to explain it.

If teachers are to respond imaginatively to the needs of sexually abused children then it helps to understand the reasons for such behaviour from the child's point of view. That means listening to children and to adult survivors. You might find it useful to read some of the anthologies listed at the end of this chapter and perhaps you can also draw on your own experiences of childhood (your own memories of keeping horrid secrets of whatever nature, your own unhappiness, your own experiences of powerlessness or physical, mental or sexual abuse). By trying to understand some of the different feelings that sexual abuse can arouse in a child we can begin to become more open to listening to children who are trying to seek help.

What if a child tells you they are being abused? What can you say? What should you do?

If a child tells you directly about sexual abuse then you will probably feel very upset and may feel panicked. Ideally, you need to think through your possible reactions before a child confides in you because it is important not to let your own emotions get in the way of giving the child effective support. Instead, a good place to start is to imagine how the child might be feeling about telling you: what are her hopes and fears?

The child will probably fear disbelief, or punishment. She might fear that you will find her disgusting and dirty. She might fear that you will blame her for what has happened. You will need to reassure her on all these points. A simple statement like 'I'm glad you told me about this' is a good place to begin. Samantha describes the positive and sensitive response of her teacher:

I knew she had a free lesson and I went to the staff room and I was shaking and I said 'Can I have a word with you please Miss?' There was a male teacher in there and she asked him to leave and I just sort of said, 'My uncle does things to me I don't like.' She said, 'What sort of things?' I says, 'He's been touching me, he's been doing things to me – you have to help me.' She sat me down and said, 'Right, I'll help you' . . . She was really good. She said, 'It isn't your fault, we'll sort it out, we'll get there,' and 'you're not the only one who's been through this.' I'd thought I was the only one and when someone actually tells you that there are other kids going through what you are going through it helps so much. And she wasn't firing questions at me all the time, she sort of gave me a question and she let me answer it in my own time. If it took me three hours then she'd stay there for three hours. And she talked to me really gently and didn't say things like 'What do you mean?'

This teacher responded immediately with sensitivity and care. The moment Samantha approached her in the staff room she asked the other (male) teacher to leave, thus creating a safer space for Samantha and indicating her readiness to listen and take her seriously. She promised help but instead of bull-dozing Samantha with decisions she clearly allied herself with the child and said 'we'll sort it out, we'll get there'. The teacher also reassured Samantha that it wasn't her fault and that she wasn't alone. There was no hint of disbelief or mistrust; the teacher did not cross-question Samantha, demand evidence or ask her to expand on anything. She did not probe but she did give her time and space to talk.

What happens next? Should I report it?

Teachers have a statutory obligation to report suspicions of abuse – you should either tell the head, or the Educational Welfare Officer, or some schools have designated members of staff to liaise with social services – there should be a school policy about the handling of any suspicions of abuse. However, many teachers feel hesitant before reporting anything through the official channels.

What if the child begs me not to tell anyone else?

Children are very fearful of the consequences of the abuse being reported. Often they have been threatened by the abuser to ensure their silence. One abuser told his victim that she would be sent to prison if anyone found out, another threatened to kill the little boy's pet dog. The child may also fear that her mother will be angry when she finds out or that the family will break up. Ask the child why she doesn't want you to tell anyone. While she may have to face some of the consequences she fears, it may be possible to reassure her on other points. However, although you may wish you could wave a magic wand and solve all the child's problems, you must not make promises you can't keep. It is a very painful decision to over-ride a child's plea for confidentiality and it is important not to bully the child or tell anyone about the abuse who is not directly concerned with helping that child (she may fear that the whole school will know and that other children will point and stare). However, teachers do have a responsibility to break through the conspiracy of silence that traps a child in an abusive situation. Some children will feel deeply betrayed if you report what they have told you, they may also feel profoundly relieved. Teachers can help to free the child from the burden of guilt by accepting reponsibility for passing on the information and getting help for the child. Explain to the child what you are going to do and take the time to reassure her where you can. While it is important not to overwhelm the child with details of all the things that could happen over the following six months you could discuss with her the very next step and explain what you are going to do.

Should I wait to make sure that the child really is being abused?
I don't want to set the wheels in motion precipitously.

You may be reading this chapter because you suspect that a child that you know is being abused. Perhaps you have not mentioned this to anyone yet because your suspicions have just been accumulating over time, perhaps you feel that you need a few days to consider what a child has told you or maybe you are trying to give the child the space to talk things through with you before taking any action that may frighten her into withdrawing her allegations. If you feel unable to act immediately you may find it useful to consult one of the help-lines anonymously or to keep written notes of what the child has said or done that has made you worry. This will help you to think through the situation and to remember the child's own words without automatically superimposing your own adult inter-pretation. You will have to judge for yourself at what point you feel it is appropriate to report your suspicions. However, remember that delays and inaction may make the child feel scared and abandoned.

Do not set yourself the task of 'proving' that there is, or is not, abuse. This can lead to the type of cross-questioning and demands for evidence that are guaranteed to make a child withdraw her allegations and your enquiries may be detrimental to any future investigation. Your role at this stage should be limited to listening to the child in as gentle and sympathetic way as possible. You are not the detective, police, judge and jury for the child.

I'm not sure what I'll be setting in motion if I report this; these things tend to 'get out of hand'.

The metaphors teachers use when considering whether to report suspicions of sexual abuse are metaphors of loss of control – horses get the bit between their teeth, rivers flood, avalanches are triggered and children get sucked into black holes. The consequences of following up suspicions of sexual abuse are complex, uncertain and often far from satisfactory. Procedures vary between areas so it is vital that good communication is established between schools and social services. Invite a social worker to come and talk to the staff about local procedure and to discuss the role of the teacher in, for instance, case conferences. Teachers have an important role to play in feeding back both information and criticisms to social services.

Doesn't intervention sometimes do more harm than good?
Besides, look at Cleveland.

Teachers often worry about the consequences of reporting abuse and, nowadays, many cite Cleveland as justification for their concern. Whatever the rights and wrongs of Cleveland the media have ensured that it has become a Medusa's head symbolizing professional error, feminist over-reaction and misguided intrusion into, and destruction of, the family. It is an image which turns many professionals to stone, inhibiting them from initiating any enquiries into suspected abuse. In the backlash reaction around Cleveland the urgent need of the abused child for outside intervention has been largely ignored. Teachers are at once intimidated and genuinely concerned about the consequences of suspecting sexual abuse. This sometimes overshadows their concern for the consequences for the child if they do *not* take any action to protect her.

'Look at Cleveland' is a phrase that has entered the English language and is used both by professionals and by abused children, but it can be used to mean very different things. Some professionals say, 'Look at Cleveland,' meaning 'We shouldn't over-react and see abuse everywhere.' Meanwhile, some abused children use the same phrase but *they* say, 'Look at Cleveland – what's the point of trying to tell anyone, they won't believe me and I'll only be sent back.' While some professionals are worried that their suspicions will be taken *too* seriously and that everything will get out of proportion, some children are worried that their allegations won't be taken seriously *enough*.

How can the school counteract abuse?

School is a place where children learn a great many formal and informal messages about obedience, humiliation and power. The school is a compulsory and hierarchical institution – as such it reinforces the powerlessness of children and their exposure to abuse. However, in so far as it can offer an alternative to the child's home environment (whether that be in a nuclear family, an extended kinship network, or an institution etc.), it can offer a way out for the child who feels trapped.

If we want children to learn strategies at school to help them resist assault we need to think about the whole school environment and how this reflects and recreates social inequalities.

1 How is bullying, sexual and racial harassment or violence dealt with, whether it is between pupils or between teachers and pupils? If a child feels such behaviour is acceptable at school then why not elsewhere? If a child feels cowed and worthless because of being called a 'lezzie' or 'nigger' how does that erode her ability to resist sexual abuse?
2 Do children get the message that they will be listened to, believed and taken seriously? How does the way in which you teach tell children how they should behave? Are children forced to obey authority without question? Are they encouraged to discuss issues and assert their own point of view?
3 What are the images of the female or male body – in textbooks, on posters, or graffitied on the loo walls. What about when girls start to develop breasts or menstruate – are they taught to be ashamed of their own bodies?
4 What about the school hierarchy and the usual gender-stratification from the female cleaners to the male head teacher? What messages is this giving about men and women and about male power?

As well as the general questioning of the school institution and teaching practice there are very specific ways of enabling children to seek help. What information and support is available to pupils at the moment?

1   Are their any posters or leaflets about phone lines like Childline or Rape Crisis? (A child might prefer to confide anonymously to an outside group than talk to a known authority figure such as a teacher.)
2   Are there relevant books in the school library or class-room shelves? (Have a look at the list at the end of the chapter.)
3   If a child wanted to talk to you about any problems, when and where would they have a chance?

Trying to create a school environment which challenges abuse and offers support to the abused can be a very isolating task. It's important to think about what support you have for yourself and what information and practical guidance you need. You might want to start by getting together with other members of staff, not just teachers but anyone who has contact with the children – the school secretary and the school nurse usually play a crucial role. Some women have found that talking about child sexual abuse brings up lots of issues about the sexual harassment they experience themselves at the hands of male members of staff and pupils – this may be a good opportunity to deal with this; you could get hold of the NUT guide-lines on sexual harassment. You could also find out what school policy, if any, exists about child sexual abuse and discuss what you think the problems are and how you would like to see things develop in the future. There are some very good initiatives starting up in schools all over the country – you might like to look at other people's articles about developing school policies on child sexual abuse [Anon. 1984; O'Hara 1988]. It's also worth obtaining a copy of the procedures for a multi-agency response on child sexual abuse from your local Area Review Committee and you could invite speakers from your nearest Rape Crisis centre as well as from social services.

Many teachers are now taking advantage of programmes, like *Kidscape*, especially designed for use in schools. These programmes help the teacher to introduce the issue of child sexual abuse in a structured and carefully thought out context. Although there are many problems with some of these training packs [Kitzinger 1988] a lot of thought has gone into making them child-centred. These packs discuss the kind of signs to look out for in an abused child, how to react when a child discloses and how to go about reporting any suspicions. They explore many issues not mentioned in this chapter and suggest ways of thinking about the situation from a child's perspective. What are we telling a child when we describe sexual molestation as 'naughty' or 'bad touch', words usually associated for children with disapproval and being told off? What are we saying if we want to help them confide in us and ask them to stay behind after class or come to the head teacher's office – situations usually associated with punishment? Some of these training packs also incorporate important preventative work with children.

Ultimately we do have to explicitly confront child sexual abuse – taking videos and training packs into the schools and working directly with the pupils. Children have to be given the information to understand what abuse is, they have to be given the words to describe what is happening to them. Angie was raped by a stranger while on a school trip; she couldn't bring herself to tell the teachers. She says:

> When you don't have words, when you don't have any meaning that you can attach to that sort of behaviour, when there isn't any permission to talk about these things . . . it was just impossible.

Having the information, the words, and the permission to talk about sexual violence can be a life line for abused children. As more and more people are prepared to talk publicly about sexual violence and teachers are beginning to use words like 'incest' and 'abuse' they are giving some children the chance to challenge sexual exploitation and to seek help. The abusers have condemned their victims to silence, the abusers try to make the secret of abuse the *child's* responsibility. The secret should not be the child's burden. It is up to those of us with more power than the abused child, where possible, to take on the responsibility of breaking the silence that protects the abuser and imprisons the child. As one survivor says:

> If someone would say the word I would talk about it, but I couldn't bring the subject up. You see, if I did, and my dad went to jail, it would be my fault. But if someone else brought it up and I talked about it, it would be their fault.
>
> (quoted in De Young 1982, p. 51)

There is then a clear need for sexual abuse to be dealt with explicitly within the school. Teachers can play a very special part in posing an overt challenge to abusers and offering hope and a way out for abused children. Education about abuse and exploitation needs to be introduced in every school. Fiona, who was sexually abused throughout her childhood, sums it up:

> Teachers need to address the issue of child abuse from the front of the classroom. If they did that it would free up the kids who are either in it or who are possible future victims . . . We are actually beginning to educate kids at five now, rightly so, because from my own experience I know you can be in the shit by four or five . . . If the teachers are open, and the kids see that, then they give the kids a chance because the kids can see that these adults are actually using these words and describing what they know to be the case . . . Teachers being open about child sexual abuse would give the message that it is not the whole of the adult population that plays these hidden games.

Note

1 Throughout this chapter I have only used original quotes with the permission of the person concerned and I have used pseudonyms for all interviewees. My work has been mainly with girls and women and, given the gender politics of sexual abuse, I have referred to any unidentifiable child as 'she'. However, boys are also assaulted and most of the issues raised apply equally to boys and girls.

Bibliography and resources

Adams, C. and Fay, J. (1981) *No More Secrets*, Impact.*

Anon (1984) 'Developing a School Policy on Sexual Abuse', *G.E.N: an anti-sexist education magazine*, Summer, No. 3, pp. 49–50.

Armstrong, L. (1987) *Kiss Daddy Goodnight*, Pocket books.†

'Breaking Silence' (1986) Albany Videos, Douglas Way, London SE8 4AG. Tel. 01 692 6322.

De Young, M. (1982) *The Sexual Victimization of Children*, McFarland & Co.

Droisen, A. and Driver, E. (1988) *Child Sexual Abuse: Some feminist perspectives*, Macmillan.

Kidscape, 82 Brook Street, London W1Y 1YG. Tel. 01 493 9845.

Kitzinger, J. (1988) 'Defending Innocence: Ideologies of childhood', *Feminist Review*, January, No. 28, pp. 16–55.

Maher, P. (1987) *Child Abuse: The educational perspective*, Blackwells, Oxford.

Morgan, L. (1987) *Megan's Secret*, Papers Inc.#

Nelson, S. (1982) *Incest: Fact and myth*, Stramullion Press.
O'Hara, M. (1988) 'Developing a Feminist School Policy on Child Sexual
   Abuse', *Feminist Review*, January, No. 28, pp. 158–62.
Riley, J. (1985) *The Unbelonging*, Women's Press.#
Spring, J. (1986) *Cry Hard and Swim*, Stramullion Press.†
Ward, E. (1984) *Father–Daughter Rape*, Women's Press.

Key
= novels/stories which could be used in school.
* = practical advice about working on sexual abuse with children.
† = including anthologies and discussions of women's experiences of child
   sexual abuse.

CHAPTER 6

'My Nan said, "Sure you're not pregnant?" ': Schoolgirl Mothers

LESLEY HOLLY

Since 1971 there have been between four and five thousand births to girls under seventeen every year. Just over one thousand of these mothers are under sixteen and should, by law, be at school. Despite their youth, schoolgirl mothers are not necessarily different from any other mothers. They need ante-natal and post-natal care, support with childcare and help to adjust to the work of motherhood. Simms and Smith (1986) point out that 'not all babies born to teenage mothers are an unwelcome burden'. Certainly for an older schoolgirl, having a baby, especially within a stable relationship, can provide a family life or an interest in the future which she may be seeking. During periods of unemployment taking care of a baby may seem a better option than the dole queue or a tedious unskilled job on the production line.

The position of the younger schoolgirl can be more difficult. A twelve or thirteen year old is not able to take the responsibility which might be encouraged in a fifteen or sixteen year old. She is more likely to have to rely on other people's decisions on her behalf. Even without the complications of pregnancy adolescence is associated with emotional upheaval. Pregnancy is likely to make the younger girl more dependent on the adults around her, possibly frustrating her desires to grow away from parents and family. However, schoolgirl mothers are individuals and their reactions to motherhood vary. Inevitably social and economic circumstances play their part. Lack of finance, lack of secure housing and lack of loving support may push any mother into a state of depression and such adverse circumstances seem unfortunately frequent in the lives of teenage mothers (Simms and Smith 1986; Coyne 1984).

On top of all the social and emotional problems that early motherhood may entail, the under sixteen year olds have the demands of
compulsory education laid upon them. The Joint Working Party
Report 'Pregnant in School' (1979) discussed how educational provision varies from one area to another. Some young mothers go back
to school after the birth. Others disappear out of the education
system often with the tacit agreement of schools and parents who
may see education as irrelevant for some girls especially if they are
nearly sixteen. Does this mean that most young mothers see
education as irrelevant? Perhaps there are some kinds of educational
environment which young mothers would enjoy and from which
they would benefit.

To find out about this I went to talk to young women and their
home tutors who met once a week at the 'Springhill Young Mothers
Group'.

Springhill Young Mothers Group

The Springhill Young Mothers Group was set up by social workers
and teachers to enable teenage mothers to meet together for social
and educational purposes. They decided that a group was needed
which would be friendly and stimulating and offer something to
young mothers who are isolated at home, unwilling to go back to
school but feeling bored and cooped up.

First the intention was to help the young mothers to get out at
least once a week and meet each other. Maureen, the worker at
Springhill House, explains why this is important.

> They mostly feel that through their pregnancy and the birth of their
> babies they are 'looked down on' by older women and made to feel
> guilty and incapable of caring for their baby.

Second there was an intention to develop educational activities for
the group but lack of space has meant that mothers and babies are
crammed together in a small room. All the attention inevitably goes
to the babies. Apart from swimming in the local pool, educational
activities have not developed.

I visited the group for about six weeks and met ten young mothers
and their babies, along with other pregnant young women, many
under the school-leaving age, and the teachers who work as their

home tutors. They meet together in a small room in a community centre. It is the only space available and the children are the focus of attention. New babies are passed around to be admired. Toddlers practise their walking skills accompanied inevitably by skirmishes over toys and the companionship of sucking each other's bottles. During the afternoon session the mothers drink tea and coffee, smoke and chat about the children. Re-telling stories about the birth of the baby has been a major feature of the group according to one of the teachers who attends. They also draw support from each other and from the staff on issues ranging from morning sickness to housing problems.

The interviews took place within this rather chaotic situation. The young women were very willing to talk about their children and their lives. This chapter is based on those interviews and conversations. I shall tell some of their stories to discuss how their pregnancies related to a variety of circumstances and emotions. Some young women wanted to be mothers but others did not. I shall ask if more sex education or better sex education might help those young women who do not seek pregnancy to avoid it. The second part of this chapter concentrates on a discussion about the kinds of educational opportunities open to young mothers. I shall consider ways in which the young mothers might continue their education which might be useful and enjoyable for them.

Some young mothers

Marlene

Marlene is seventeen and her daughter Mary is eighteen months old. Marlene was in a children's home when she became pregnant. Her adoptive parents had split up and her father re-married, but relations were strained between her and her stepmother. She explains: 'I was fifteen. I was in the children's home because I hadn't got on well with my stepmother.' Marlene's boyfriend David also lived in the home when they began their relationship. Marlene had never considered contraception. 'I wasn't using anything when I fell with her. I never thought I'd get pregnant.'

When she told the workers in the home about her pregnancy all the options were discussed including abortion. 'The people in the home kept saying you've got three options: abortion, having her or adoption. Well, I didn't want adoption and I knew I want her anyway so I didn't take any notice of what anybody said. I went on and had her.'

During this time Marlene kept on going to school and she got a lot of support from her teachers but she put up with hostility from other pupils. 'There were people at school, who were really bitchy because I was pregnant. There was a lot of trouble there. My friends were very supportive. I tried to cover it up for a while. I got so big that I couldn't in the end.'

Before the birth Marlene left school and she had Jenny as a home tutor until the baby was born. She now lives in a flat with David and is planning to get married and possibly have another baby. As she is seventeen she has withdrawn from education altogether.

Tracey

Tracey is sixteen and has Simon who is eight months old. At fifteen Tracey ran away from home when her mother's boyfriend moved in. Tracey said he was often violent towards her. She had a long-standing relationship with her boyfriend Keith who was twenty-one. She left home and they lived with his parents and she got pregnant. She says she was pleased: 'I did want the baby. I was very pleased about it.'

Throughout the pregnancy Tracey had Jenny as her home tutor and Jenny gave some of the emotional support that Tracey needed to tell her mother about the pregnancy. 'I asked her advice about what to tell my mum. She supported me a lot.' Tracey now lives in a council house with Keith and Simon and she suggests that having a baby enabled her to establish the family life she wanted and needed. 'I always wanted children early. I had him when I was just sixteen.'

Lucy

Lucy is sixteen and now lives in a council flat with her son John who is eighteen months old. Lucy was fourteen when she got pregnant. At school Lucy and her friends used to stay away from unpopular lessons. 'The crowd I was with used to go into school but never ended up going into hardly any of the lessons. You'd sit in the toilet and have a fag, have a natter. When I did go it was all right. The teachers I had were nice.'

Lucy doesn't remember the sex education classes, so she knew little about contraception. 'I didn't end up turning up. In the toilet for a fag, I expect.' She got pregnant after a party. The father was a childhood friend who lived nearby but he was not someone she wanted as a regular boyfriend. During the pregnancy she managed to avoid feeling too anxious by pretending it was not happening: 'I was worried, scared but other than that . . . I didn't use to think about it.' Consequently she did not tell anybody and everybody thought she was just getting fatter. Her dad said she ought to go on a diet.' My dad said for every pound I lose I'd get a fiver.'

The week before she had the baby Lucy went on a horse-riding holiday in Wales with the school. Still nobody knew. She was in the bath at home one evening when her waters broke so she wrote a note and gave it to her little sister to take downstairs to her mother. She wrote, 'Dear Mum, come upstairs I'm having a baby.' Her mother rang the ambulance and Lucy had John two hours later.

After the birth she went back to school. She would go in at lunchtime and finish about two o'clock. Then she realised she was only duplicating what she was doing at home. 'All I was doing was childcare and I've already had enough experience.'

Sally came to Lucy's home as her tutor. Lucy was her first schoolgirl mother so she was rather unsure about the approach to adopt. Lucy enjoyed her visits. 'She always took me out, to the park or to the zoo, and we talked.' Sally explains, 'They always say, "You're not a teacher. You don't teach us anything." '

Lucy now lives on her own with John in a small council flat. She doesn't have any contact with John's father who has moved away. Lucy has some free time as her mother babysits and her father takes care of John every weekend. How does she view motherhood a year later?

'If I could do it again I would have made sure I never had a baby but he came along so . . .'

Sandra

Sandra is fifteen. She has just moved into a foster home with three-month-old baby Ivan. Sandra was fourteen when she became pregnant. The baby's father Alex is nineteen and Sandra has known him for two years. Before the pregnancy she had lived with her father and stepmother but she didn't get on with her stepmother. Once she knew she was pregnant she went to live with her grandmother. 'I kept arguing and fighting with her [stepmother]. I knew I was pregnant and I didn't want to lose it. I moved to my Nan's – I knew I was safe there.'

Sandra did not know how to cope with the pregnancy so she pretended everything was normal. Before the Easter when she had the baby Sandra helped her Nan move house. She was then five months pregnant. Sandra says, 'I helped her move wardrobes and beds. I done a six-and-a-half-mile cross-country at six months pregnant.' Her Nan did suspect, however. Sandra explains that her Nan kept saying, 'Sure you're not pregnant?' to which Sandra always replied, 'I'm not pregnant.' Inevitably her Nan 'found out in the end though'.

She had the baby in hospital but she would not go in until *EastEnders* was over. '[The contractions] came every ten minutes but I wouldn't leave the house until *EastEnders* was finished. Then I had my cup of tea. When I finally got there I was over half-way gone.'

First Sandra and the baby lived with Alex's mother but they quarrelled. Then she lived with Alex and his father but recently Sandra has had arguments with them both. Alex helped to get Sandra into a foster home. Then he decided that Sandra should hand over the baby to him because he said she was an unfit mother.

Sally, who is Sandra's home tutor, sees her role as helping Sandra to make the best decisions for herself. 'Sandra is very vulnerable. She allowed Alex to tell her he should have care and custody and she believes him . . . she needs somebody right beside her all the time saying, "Sandra! No! You must keep the baby. He's yours." '

Anna

Anna lives in a flat with her baby, Michael, and Peter her boyfriend. She became pregnant when she was fifteen. She had been staying away from school. 'I was pregnant in January, but I hadn't been to school since November. I just stayed away.' Peter is twenty-one. They had split up but got back together when Anna was in hospital having the baby. Sally, the home tutor, visits Anna two or three times a week and Anna sees her as a friend. Sally explains, 'She'd like me to come every day. We're good friends.'

These young women have some things in common. They all have babies and they all smoke. They all live in council housing and none are in employment. Apart from these similarities their lives are very different in the ways that they can tap into support networks. Some of the young women in the group have stable relationships and live with their partner. Often the man is working and supports the mother and baby. Of the young women who live alone or with their family Lucy can rely on her family for babysitting and extra money. Sandra is in the worst situation. The council cannot re-house her in a flat as she is under age. She has to stay in foster homes. The other young women who have their own homes find life easier, although most have some financial problems.

The concerns of all the young mothers centre on caring for the baby, housing and finance. For the reluctant mothers of the group who had not planned a pregnancy it is relevant to ask if these domestic cares could have been delayed by a better programme of sex education, especially concerning contraception. In the next section I shall consider some aspects of sex education and abortion counselling.

Contraception

In our society motherhood at a young age is generally considered inappropriate and there has been a considerable body of writing and research which discusses the potential hazards from pregnancy to both mother and child. However it is possible that problems relate to social class rather than the youth of the mother as most teenage pregnancies occur in predominantly working-class families (Reid 1982). Certainly babies born to young mothers are at greater risk of being underweight at birth. Simms and Smith (1986) suggest that 'still births, neonatal deaths, post natal deaths and infant deaths are all higher for teenagers than for the 20–24 age group (OPCS 1982).'

The social consequences of early motherhood usually include severe restrictions on choices about jobs and future prospects (admittedly already restricted). As very young mothers with babies frequently come from overcrowded houses and materially less advantaged families (Wilson 1980), this means that the young mother may more easily fall into a cycle of deprivation in poor housing with few employment prospects.

For these reasons the avoidance of early pregnancy for the majority of young women, who do not want it, should be a priority. However, the solutions are not straightforward. Improving the options available to young women and developing economic opportunities are part of essential reforms if motherhood is not to be seen as the major source of competence and value for young women.

Inevitably in the current atmosphere of individualism it is the campaigns which aim to change people rather than the system which gain support. This brings us to sex education.

The campaign against AIDS has set the need for barrier contraception in a new perspective and if people use condoms it will undoubtedly affect the number of teenage pregnancies. A simple solution to reduce teenage pregnancies would appear to be more effective sex education in school but unfortunately increased sex education does not necessarily mean an increase in pupil knowledge or a willingness to use contraception at the appropriate moment. A number of studies have discussed how there is no simple relationship between the provision of information about contraception and its subsequent use (Schofield 1973; Black 1979). Christine Farrell (1978) found that forty-six per cent of her sample were unprotected at their first experience of sexual intercourse. Since Farrell's research the situation has deteriorated since parental consent is now necessary before a doctor can prescribe the birth control pill.

Of the young women in the Springhill Young Mothers Group, all had the opportunity to attend sex education lessons at school but none had considered issues about 'contraception' for themselves in advance of first experiences of sexual intercourse. They did not use contraception because they could not believe that pregnancy could happen to them. Apart from Tracey's all the pregnancies were unplanned.

Michelle: You don't realize the importance of it really. You just take it for granted that you're not going to [get pregnant].

Jane believed that because she had a long-standing sexual relationship and had not got pregnant she was safe for the future. 'We hadn't been using anything for ages and I thought probably it's all right.'

Lucy and Marlene both thought that because they had short-term relationships they would not get pregnant.

Lucy: This was a sort of one-off thing.
Marlene: I did not think it would ever happen to me. We'd only been sleeping together a few weeks.

They did have some criticisms of sex education in school.

Jane: It [contraception] was all done in a couple of lessons.
Linda: You need more detail of what happens. They say if you go with a fella, go on the pill . . . You need more detail, much more detail.

Not only do these young women need more 'detail' and more understanding of all the options open to them but they also need space and time to discuss issues about sexuality including contraception. Those courses which regard sex education as concerned only with giving information may be failing the young women who need the space to relate the information to their own sexual needs.

As Michelle, one of the young mothers at Springhill, explained: 'They don't go into a lot of detail. They just tell you what things are . . . they just rush through it.'

What these young women seemed to need was contraceptive counselling which gave space for their own experiences rather than just the information. In the United States where some School Based Health Clinics have been set up, many of which provide counselling and contraceptives, there is evidence that pupils are more likely to postpone sexual intercourse and contraception is used more reliably. Fears that these clinics would increase promiscuity have been allayed. Petchesky suggests that the availability of these services enables young women to feel more in control of their sexual futures: 'With a sense of sexual agency and not necessarily urgency, teen girls may be less likely to use or be used by pregnancy' (Petchesky 1984 quoted in Fine 1988).

Increasingly young men have also attended the clinics, viewing contraception as a shared responsibility (Fine 1988). In Britain government campaigns to alert the population to the spread of the HIV virus may increase this sense of responsibility in young men. However, for the young women at Springhill it was all too late. Contraception was never discussed between them and their partners.

Marlene: We never talked about it really.
Lucy: He never said nothing.

In Britain there is no equivalent to the School Based Health Clinic. There are Well Women Clinics and Birth Control Clinics but they are attended by a minority of all sexually active teenage women. It is sex education in schools which is supposed to provide access to this knowledge. Sex education is accepted as an aspect of public schooling. Recent government attempts to bring it under the influence of school governors no doubt reflect a desire to gain greater control of such courses, locating them within the context of family life and traditional values.

Clearly sex education as it is currently organized is not sufficient to substantially reduce teenage pregnancy rates and it is unrealistic to expect it to do so, especially if contraception is covered in one or two lessons with an emphasis on impersonal information.

Abortion

About 37,000 teenage girls have abortions every year. The proportion of conceptions terminated by abortion has considerably increased for the under twenty year olds. The statistics published for 1984 showed that over 1000 young women under fifteen had their pregnancies terminated by legal abortion and there were more than 36,500 terminations for young women aged between fifteen and nineteen.

A study by the Policy Studies Institute (1985) discussed late abortions and pointed out that as many as a third of under sixteen year olds and a fifth of sixteen to nineteen year olds did not go to the doctor until ten weeks pregnant. This then becomes a problem because of possible delays in health service procedures.

In their report 'Late Abortions in England and Wales' (1984) the Royal College of Obstetricians and Gynaecologists pointed to avoidable delays in the health service before referral or between assessment and admission in a significant proportion of late abortions. This means that any change in the time limits in the abortion laws will put younger women most at risk of unwanted motherhood.

There is great regional variation in facilities for abortion and the outcome of teenage pregnancies varies widely around the country. The Birth Control Trust points out that in London a much higher proportion of young women have an abortion, while in the northern region more women get married when they are pregnant (*Abortion Review*, Feb. 1986).

However, abortion was not the choice for these young women at the Springhill Young Mothers Group. Some were positively against it.

> *Michelle*: I'm against it. I don't think there's any reason to take a life.
> *Jane*: I knew if I had an abortion I would have regretted it all my life.

It would be unrealistic to expect the anti-abortion lobby to value women's lives as it values the lives of the unborn but this is also a strong cultural thread in our society. It is not surprising that, with limited employment prospects and with the cultural emphasis on motherhood as the natural future for all women, these young women consider abortion wrong. However, in many cases it is a choice which is made against very few alternatives.

Some other young mothers are not opposed to abortion. For young women like Lucy abortion might have been a possibility if she had admitted to herself that she was pregnant. This passive drift into motherhood is typical of many young mothers according to a social worker at the centre. 'Many young women can't consider abortion because they can't admit they are pregnant.'

Young working-class women can be virtually powerless to make decisions in their own lives. Without money or future prospect they have little sense of being entitled to much from life. If they admitted to pregnancy they would have to do something and that is not necessarily very easy. Social attitudes to abortion make it a difficult option to consider. Simms and Smith (1986) discuss a number of cases where young women have been afraid to turn to their GP for contraceptive advice. It is not surprising that many also feel unable to discuss a possible abortion with a GP. Direct access to abortion clinics through the National Health Service would undoubtedly ease many of these anxieties because there would be no inter-mediary hurdles to negotiate.

Many of the young mothers really want their babies and enjoy them as the focus of their lives. For them abortion is inappropriate and they have as much right to motherhood as any other woman.

Back to school

Having failed to use contraceptives and having been unwilling or unable to secure an abortion, the pregnant schoolgirl must face motherhood. This may include finding ways of juggling education with childcare. What kind of educational opportunities should be provided for schoolgirl mothers? The answer must depend on the young woman herself. Someone who has been truanting from school will have different demands from girls who have ambitions to take exams and gain qualifications.

Local Education Authorities vary considerably in policies which respond to the needs of pregnant schoolgirls and schoolgirl mothers. There is a clear legal requirement for girls to receive education until the age of sixteen. This can take a number of forms. Home tuition is available in theory, for all girls who are not attending school before and after childbirth. However, in their report 'Pregnant in School'

(1979), the Joint Working Party on Schoolgirl Mothers found a great variation in services from one area to another. Home tuition was often unavailable or spasmodic.

There are also facilities for pregnant schoolgirls and schoolgirl mothers in Special Education Units in some areas. According to the report, at least one unit places pregnant schoolgirls with mentally and physically handicapped children who also cannot attend school. This linking of schoolgirl pregnancy with subnormality and handicap suggests an unfortunate extension of the idea of handicap.

Other units cater solely for pregnant schoolgirls and schoolgirl mothers. Many units operate with health services to ensure that girls have ante-natal and post-natal care. Health care of the babies is also included and there may be links with the social services.

In the Joint Working Party report opposition was expressed to these units and the report suggests it is desirable for girls to return to school as soon as possible: 'any significant interruption of the education of pregnant schoolgirls or schoolgirl mothers is likely to deprive them of the opportunity to realise their full potential and will therefore have repercussions throughout their lives.'

The high value which the working party set on school education is not really echoed in the experiences of young women at the Springhill group. Many had found school to be largely irrelevant to their interests even before pregnancy. For these girls, education could hardly be said to guarantee future work prospects. The desire to remain at school was noticeably lacking among the young women in the group. However, one local school had produced a policy document on pregnant schoolgirls suggesting that they be treated in the same way as a pregnant teacher. This school has a crèche nearby, linked with a community centre, and the document suggests ways in which the role of mother and schoolgirl could be made compatible by using the crèche facilities. The document is very recent and as yet no schoolgirl mother has returned to this school to test the policy.

Although other subjects such as childbirth and contraception had been easily discussed in the Springhill Young Mothers Group, conversations about return to school seemed quite inappropriate. Even for Sandra, who was the youngest member of the group, pressing concerns such as the care of the baby, the instability of her housing arrangements and her lack of financial support pushed educational issues into the background. All the other young women in the group lived independently of their families and were far more self-reliant

than the average fifteen or sixteen year old. It is difficult to see what
school might have to offer to them. Having attained adult status
through the experiences and responsibilities of motherhood, school
seemed a very juvenile environment. Many of these young mothers
had suffered verbal abuse from other pupils in their class while
pregnant. Their memories of school were not therefore necessarily
happy ones.

In the area of Springhill the home tutor system is well developed
and all the young women in the group had home tuition while they
were pregnant or after the birth. Many had established close relationships with their home tutors Sally or Jenny. The advantage of
home tuition is that the tutor can design a programme around the
needs of the young woman and this flexibility is essential. Their
educational needs are varied and Sally regards each of her young
mothers very differently. Sally at this time tutored Jane who wanted
to take O levels. 'Jane is desperate to do her O levels. She is so
self-motivated. She's bright and she's got her family behind her. She
works all the time – she is the other extreme. I work with her or I
look after the baby while she studies. My job there is to liaise
between her and the school.'

Other young mothers are often more in need of stimulation and
stability because their home circumstances are insecure. Sally
explains: 'Because of home circumstances I am often the only person
who is steady, who the younger mother can depend on. She knows
I'll come every week. She knows my views will always be the same
. . . often I just hope for some kind of maturing. Just support them
while they mature.'

The kind of learning and teaching is different for different girls.
Sally takes them out on trips and 'educational visits' and she talks to
them and helps them to make decisions. 'It's conversation, talking
about the baby, giving reassurance, making them feel confident . . .
older people they see as being critical . . . it's just being there saying,
"Yes, I know how you feel," and telling them that these feelings are
all right.'

Clearly the kind of support which a home tutor like Sally can give
is invaluable to some young women. But some of their problems are
intractable and Sally can only give limited support, as with Sandra
who has been moved from one place to another and has never known
security. 'I've been her home tutor since before Ivan was born – her
circumstances have never been right. I don't know what I would
want to happen to Sandra now.'

Jenny also points to the insecurity in the lives of some of her young mothers. Sometimes she has nowhere to take them for a lesson. 'Quite often the home isn't a suitable place for tutoring in any way or the girl is moving from home to home because nobody actually wants her and home tutors seem to spend most of their time driving round in cars looking for somewhere to take them.'

Young mothers unit

To overcome some of the problems facing young mothers who are still of school age it has been proposed that the Springhill Young Mothers Group should be absorbed into a Young Mothers Unit which would cater for all pregnant schoolgirls and schoolgirl mothers in the area. They would be collected daily and there would be facilities for sewing, cooking, photography, sport, talks on child-care and other subjects which the young women could suggest themselves. The babies would be cared for in a crèche.

Clearly it would not be appropriate for all young mothers and young women in this group would not want to go every day but most seemed interested when the plan was suggested. Even Tracey and Marlene, who were old enough to refuse to participate, seemed interested.

> *Tracey*: I think it's a good idea, getting together to do something.
> *Marlene*: Yes, I'd go.
> *Lucy*: As long as it's not too educational. You know.

What seemed to be lacking in the plans was training for future work.

Experience in the United States suggests that some kinds of vocational training helps to give young mothers a sense of competence and optimism about their personal worth in the world. This is particularly the case if they can acquire skills which will have an economic value. They are less likely to see motherhood as a major source of identity and this affects attitudes towards contraception and abortion. Writing about young women's training programmes in New York, Michelle Fine comments: 'attitudes towards contraception and abortion shifted once they [young women] acquired a set of vocational skills, a sense of social entitlement and a sense of personal competence.' (Fine 1988, p. 47)

The Young Mothers Unit which will replace the Springhill group will undoubtedly provide a warm supportive environment with some educational opportunities. However, liaising with training schemes to give young mothers marketable skills and providing childcare while they do it would also seem to be a very appropriate way of helping those young women who wanted to do so, to step into a future which might include employment and a steady income. This would help to combat the problems raised by Lucy: 'I would like to get a job when he [John] is at nursery. I'm not trained for anything. 'Spect I'll work in a shop.'

This young mothers group is in an area where there are employment prospects especially in relation to new technology. Many other young women are trained for skilled work so why not some of these young mothers? Part of the reason why this is not suggested might be the deep resistance to women in paid employment while they have very young children – the idea that mothers should be at home with their children and that is a sufficient future for women. In three years time all these babies could be in nursery schools and the young women will be faced with the choice of having more children or finding employment. Having left school at fifteen or sixteen will not be a great asset in employment terms unless the young women have been able to keep up with their education or have acquired other skills. Obviously this kind of continuing education is not appropriate for all young mothers. Some do not have any wish to find employment and others are in insecure and vulnerable situations. For some, however, it would be appropriate and valuable to have vocational training.

Conclusion

All the young women at the Springhill Young Mothers group expressed their pleasure in their children and despite the problems of motherhood enjoyed their company. However, the young women who were reluctant mothers might have avoided pregnancy if a more effective system of contraceptive counselling had been available which allowed them to explore the issues in the contexts of their lives.

For young mothers with a commitment to care for their children it is clearly appropriate to rethink educational provision to ensure its relevance to their lives. This does not mean simply cooking and childcare although these subjects might have a place in the curriculum. At the moment educational provision is minimal and schoolgirl mothers suffer, as many mothers do, from the isolation and boredom of being confined all day with a small child. There are strong grounds for demanding better educational support for schoolgirl mothers and that support should be flexible and varied to cope with different needs.

These young mothers say on many occasions that they want to be involved in activities which interest them. Overall the system must clearly be flexible. The Joint Working Party (1979) pointed to the importance of support and acceptance for any young woman who wants to return to school. For those who do not want to return, some kind of continuing education with other young mothers could prove stimulating and supportive as long as the young women are treated like women, not schoolgirls and are able to negotiate their own curriculum, or to be involved in training for paid employment.

Bibliography

Abortion Review (1986) no. 21, Birth Control Trust, February 1986.

Allen, I. (1985) *Counselling Services for Sterilisation, Vasectomy and Termination of Pregnancy*, Policy Studies Institute.

Black, D. (1979) 'Antecedent Factors in Teenage Pregnancy', *Fertility and Contraception*, 3, No. 4, October, pp. 59–64.

Coyne, A. (1984) 'School Girl Mothers', Research Report No. 2, Health Educational Council.

Farrell, C. (1978) *My Mother Said*, Routledge and Kegan Paul.

Fine, M. (1988) Sexuality Schooling and Adolescent Females: The missing discourse of desire, *Harvard Educational Review*, Vol. 58, No. 1.

Joint Working Party Report (1979) 'Pregnant in School', National Council for One Parent Families and Community Development Trust.

Reid, D. (1982) 'School Sex Education and the Causes of Unintended Teen-age Pregnancies – A review', *Health Educational Journal*, Vol. 41, No. 1.

Royal College of Obstetricians (1984) *Late abortions in England and Wales*, Royal College of Obstetricians.

Schofield, M. (1973) *The Sexual Behaviour of Young Adults*, Allen Lane.

Simms M. and Smith C. (1986) *Teenage Mothers and Their Partners*, HMSO.

Wilson (1980) 'Antecedents of Adolescent Pregnancy', *Journal of Biosocial Science*, 12, pp. 141–52.

Wynn, M. and G. (1975) *Prevention of Handicap and the Health of Women*, Routledge and Kegan Paul.

Reflecting on Our Experiences

CHAPTER 7

Girls' Experience of Menstruation in School

SHIRLEY PRENDERGAST

Introduction

Speak to almost any woman and you will find that they have the most vivid memory of their first period. Talking to friends and acquaintances recently, as part of thinking about and writing this chapter, I was amazed by the immediacy of the detail and emotional clarity of the remembered experience – for some now recalling an event twenty years or more ago. No doubt if I had talked to fathers or brothers they too might have had a trace memory of that event as bystanders, if only a recollection of a strange silence or change in the young women around them that indicated that *something* had happened. This curious conjunction of a vivid and precipitous event shrouded in a kind of fateful secrecy is an experience that I assumed only women of a certain age had, for surely younger women and girls today would not be caught in the same contradictions women had twenty years ago. In those days of the eleven plus, sex education was little evident in the way that it now is and has to be, as part of every school curriculum, with menstruation taught to both girls and boys probably several times over in their academic careers (Allen 1987). However, the present focus in sex education is very much on contraception, teenage pregnancy and sexually transmitted diseases, while menstruation, although a part of 'the sexual', seems to be marked by a particular kind of neglect or lack of interest. In school it is routinely covered, usually in biology, in the first year or so, followed by a later talk or film, often financed by sanitary wear manufacturers, given to girls only (Allen 1987). This coverage, its forms, its framework, and its content, is rarely discussed when school sex education undergoes its regular scrutiny in media and political circles, and the teaching has changed little, as far as I can see over the past decade or so. Interestingly too, the debates, largely initiated by feminists, about gender and sexuality in school in the widest possible sense, are also strangely silent on the issue of menstruation. At the same time we all know how the experience of menstruation, for adult women at least, can carry with it a significant negative weight: it is generally socially invisible and is considered an unacceptable topic of conversation. It may be used to ascribe to femininity or womanhood associations of physical uncleanliness, cyclic irregularity, moodiness, unreliability and lack of emotional control or worse (see Weideger 1977, Laws, Hey and Eagan 1985). Therefore of all issues in school sex education menstruation is perhaps one of the most pressingly realistic – it is one of the issues taught in school that most girls will certainly regularly experience while they are there, and many girls will depend upon school to supplement the information they already have about it.

Menstruation also comes at a key time of transition for many girls, from primary school into the more adult world of secondary school – a transition that we know is already full of anxiety for girls and boys alike (Measor and Woods 1984). Alongside unfamiliar routines, structures and subjects come new hidden curricula, in which gender differences, already evident in primary school, may take on new forms and power. It is in this context that girls must first learn to publicly 'manage' the experience of menstruation outside of home, and outside of the familiar resources and privacy that home might offer. It is suggested in this chapter that alongside the formal curriculum of teaching about menstruation goes an even more powerful source of learning that comes via the way that menstruation is itself dealt with in school. It is this hidden curriculum that I want to explore. The material drawn upon here is taken from a preliminary pilot study designed to explore some of the issues in a relatively open-ended fashion, which will lead, to a more focused study in 1989.

The pilot concentrated on accounts of menstruation at two points in the recent experience of girls of fourteen to sixteen. The first was their *recalled experience of their first period* (remembered from their present vantage point), on average two to three years previously; the second was their *present experience now* (1987). These two points were chosen deliberately, for they cover that time when girls are moving to, or settling into, secondary schooling, and the early years in which option choices are being made. It seemed illuminating to look at the overlap of these events with definitions of becoming 'adult', or 'properly female', that are so often used to frame menstruation for young women, placing them in the material context that schools provide for dealing with this topic. It is during this time too, that girls themselves learn to 'cope' with menstruation, the resonances and images of which may continue to set a pattern into adult life.

The accounts used here come from girls in secondary schools in East Anglia. In all forty-two girls between the ages of fourteen and sixteen were interviewed in small groups of five or six, and subsequently asked to fill in a brief questionnaire covering part of the material discussed in the interview. Interviews took place in school in school time. They were primarily intended to explore unknown territory and were therefore as open-ended as possible. The questionnaire was designed to substantiate some of the issues raised in the interview. As a control some girls were given the questionnaire without being interviewed. In all, fifty completed questionnaires were collected, twenty from the latter group and thirty from the former. Each group interview lasted at least half an hour and several were longer, limited by the time available in school. Because the focus was girls' experiences no attempts have been made to correlate these with the actual policy or provision of each school.

Telling stories

The girls came in small groups of five or six, rather nervous and apprehensive at first. Luckily we usually had a quiet room and nobody came in, in itself, in my experience, an unusual occurrence in a busy secondary school. Stories of one kind or another seem to attach themselves to this topic once you declare an interest or speak openly. The stories began almost as soon as I entered school. Several women teachers had stories of their own to tell about male staff and their 'Stone Age' attitudes, about facilities in school and staffroom jokes. There were girls' stories about boys, about embarrassing accidents, about girls who dared to speak publicly about periods to a male teacher, and of course the archetypal story about 'when I first started my periods'. These are very like 'stories' I heard from friends of my own age; stories that by the intensity of their telling also tell us something about the subject matter itself.

Here I want to describe in as straightforward a way as possible, through some of the 'stories' and some of the information gathered via the questionnaire, girls' experiences of menstruation in school at the present time. The accounts are mostly taken from the latter part of the data – that on girls' *current* experiences in school. Girls were asked to think about physical, emotional and practical aspects of periods, and to focus particularly on the school setting. Although these aspects will be described separately, in the interviews and in the questionnaire it was clear that such distinctions were blurred for girls themselves: they described themselves as being fed up or depressed about the practical aspects or the pain as much as feeling depressed *per se*. Something of this interlocking of symptoms and practicalities and their effects can be seen in the quotes used here. It can also be perceived in the retrospective nature of their accounts, for as experience changed so too did coping strategies in school; new features arose as others were overcome. As girls talked, many features of early experience emerged in this way: things that they had been anxious about as well as things that still did cause anxiety but for which solutions had been found as they had become more experienced. In girls' accounts of symptoms and practicalities at the present time, then, we can see common threads of experience that link them to the early days.

I feel so bad that everybody knows

At the time of this study the majority of girls were fifteen or over (36 out of the 50). Given the average age of menarche at twelve and a half (in this sample), this suggests that most had established a more regular cycle, and that most would be ovulating by now. Ovulation may bring with it a range of additional symptoms, including pain and headaches, swollen stomach, and feelings of depression or fatigue. In fact many of these changes were reflected in girls' experiences as they recorded them in the questionnaire and spoke about them in the interview.

Recognizing that not all women get negative or distressing symptoms around or during their periods (and indeed some women report feeling 'better' or with more energy at this time) the question of symptoms was approached as neutrally as possible in the interview by asking 'how they felt generally at this time' (and by providing a range of precoded possibilities in the questionnaire, as well as more open-ended questions). Perhaps the most striking thing was the extent to which girls reported negative symptoms as they got older, particularly in comparison with what they remembered of early experiences. Their responses in the questionnaire were as follows:

Table 1

Feeling better than usual	0
Just the same as usual	2
A bit 'off colour'	6
Spots	16
Can't concentrate	16
Swollen tummy	26
Stomach ache or headache	40
Feeling depressed	42
'Other' (bad tempered, moody, grouchy)	20

In total then the fifty girls who filled in the questionnaire reported 166 symptoms between them, an average of three plus symptoms per girl. In practice the clusters of symptoms were more polarized, with almost half reporting four or more symptoms before or during their periods.

The most common symptoms were physical – headache or stomach ache, in combination with some kind of mood change – not being able to concentrate, feeling depressed or bad tempered. Often it was this combination of physical and emotional effects that caused the most distress. As one girl, who reported four symptoms (a bit off colour, headache/stomach ache, spots and not being able to concentrate) noted, the most difficult thing about being in school is:

> . . . that while you have pains in your stomach, head and everywhere else you have teachers telling you what to do, to behave and get on with your work. I find it hard to actually concentrate on my work. They don't know what is happening and how you feel. One day I sat a whole day trying to concentrate which was impossible. I wish teachers could actually sense you are not well so they could be more sympathetic.

Another noted that:

> Periods are the worst time of the month. I feel so bad that everybody knows, I don't have to say. I feel big and uncomfortable and just have rows with everybody, even my best friends.

This girl had noted five symptoms, and said that her periods were 'awful and painful because I always have a heavy period'.

The ways in which girls assessed their symptoms is of course problematic and must relate in part to what they expected their periods to be like at the start; and how individuals cope with distress or pain varies tremendously. Some of the girls, while reporting several symptoms, for example, did not experience them as 'too much', but these were in the minority. Twelve girls felt that although periods were 'horrible' they were 'natural' – and that somehow they were 'worth it' in order to have a baby. For example one girl recorded feeling 'depressed, getting very annoyed with friends, having a swollen tummy and stomach ache' wished that periods 'wouldn't be so painful and wouldn't make me so annoyed and cross, and stop you having a good time', but says they mean 'knowing you can have a child'. Another six girls seemed to feel that although difficult periods are just something women and girls are burdened with and must overcome, as one of them expressed it (describing symptoms of stomach ache, swollen tummy, spots and feeling depressed and moody):

> They are part of life, and something you just have to accept, like it or not!

In the main though, the majority of girls saw menstruation as mostly negative to be endured and this seemed constant whether they had few or many symptoms.

'I talk to friends the most because they understand'

Given this negativity, the amount of symptoms described and the numbers who had both physical and emotional effects, it is interesting to see who girls felt they could talk to about menstruation. The question of talking to others was explored twice. First they were asked *who would be 'easy' or 'difficult' to talk to* if they needed support, and secondly who they *actually* told about the symptoms they experienced. In terms of the first question – people who it might be difficult or easy to talk to about menstruation – all girls named at least two groups of 'sympathetic' people who they felt it would be 'easy' to talk to, and this usually included someone at school as well as at home.

In general only two girls felt that there was nobody in school who it would be easy to talk to. Nevertheless the school nurse was seen as easier to talk to than female teachers – only twenty-eight girls out of

Table 2

48 girls said it would be easy to talk to	friends at home or at school
46 "	" mothers or stepmothers
40 "	" the school nurse
28 "	" a female teacher at school
14 "	" sisters
4 "	" dad
1 "	" male teacher at school

fifty named female teachers in this way. Turning to the category of 'difficult' to talk to:

Table 3

48 girls said it would be difficult to talk to	male teacher
48 "	" brothers
46 "	" fathers
20 "	" female teachers
10 "	" school nurse
4 "	" mothers

It is clear that men in general were seen as taboo confidants for girls of this age, although four girls had talked to fathers and found them kind and sympathetic, and one girl had talked to a male teacher at school. As we have already seen, just over half of the girls (28) felt it would be easy to talk to female teachers, but almost as many felt it would be difficult. Their uneasiness about telling even female teachers in school is emphasized if we look at the interview data, for it was often the same (few) individual women teachers being named by pupils, rather than 'women teachers' more generally. Male teachers whenever possible were carefully avoided in this respect.

The girls were then asked if they *actually* told anybody, at home or at school, about the symptoms and effects that they reported having at the present time, and if so what help or advice they were given. Most girls had told someone about their experiences, forty-two told a mother or stepmother at home, and in the school context thirty girls had also spoken to someone. In school, however, we found that girls talked to friends and only in a few cases had a school nurse been confided in, beyond the practical buying of pads in an emergency, while some girls had talked to a sympathetic female teacher.

What emerges very strongly from both questionnaires and interviews is girls' sense that there is little that can be done to help them at this time so it is hardly worth asking: a fatalism that comes through too in the kinds of advice and help that are actually given when girls do ask, for example:

> Well there's not a lot she can do, is there, anyway? Just shoves you an aspirin and says it's natural pain, so you've got to grin and bear it.

> My mum is sympathetic: she understands why I'm so moody but there's nothing she can do. I talk to friends the most because they understand best.

'Sympathy' and 'a tablet' are the commonest responses to girls who do talk about how they feel (although twenty girls noted that the response they got was 'nothing' or 'not a lot'), and these would seem to coincide with the symptoms most reported by girls, feeling 'fed up' and 'depressed' or having stomach cramps. Perhaps not surprisingly the issue that girls asked most questions about in the interview and in the questionnaire and about which they noted they would like more information was that of 'dealing with pain'. Although many had heard that the pill regulates periods and lessens pain, for almost all girls in the interview the pill as a solution was out of the question. 'Going on the pill' was seen as a dangerous and 'unnatural' course of action, and, moreover, one that had other implications. 'Going on the pill' might be interpreted by parents, teachers or friends as evidence of being, or wishing to be, sexually active, or of being a 'slag', images that girls desperately wanted to avoid, even if their doctor would prescribe the pill, or parents agree to it in the first place.

Consequences: The experience of menstruation at school

So far girls' experiences of menstrual symptoms have been described and who they felt able to talk to about them, at school and at home. Many of the fourteen to sixteen year olds were experiencing both physical and emotional effects regularly and their overall feelings about menstruation were generally negatively rather than positively orientated, although many girls recognized the 'future reproduction' argument in their favour. Girls were highly selective in who they felt they could talk to, and in the school context male teachers and boys were usually ruled out, the major contacts being via home or friends. The focus of the study was to explore how girls felt they 'managed' in school, and to look at how girls perceived the general attitudes and facilities offered to them at this time, and it is this aspect this is described below.

Girls had a great deal to say about this issue. The group interviews, lively and animated anyway, became particularly noisy at this point, as everybody tried to talk at once. Many girls too made more lengthy comments about their own needs and experiences in the questionnaire replies. These comments are divided up under a number of themes:

(a) Worries and embarrassment
(b) Practical arrangements: school facilities
(c) Being in lessons: games and talking to teachers
(d) Feeling ill: missing school or 'sitting at the back'.

(a) Worries and embarrassment

Girls were asked about things that might worry or embarrass them around the experience of menstruation in school in both the interviews and the questionnaire. In the questionnaire a number of issues were listed, together with a space where girls could add any extra themes of their own.

Table 4: Numbers of girls responding 'yes' to the following questions

Do you ever get worried or embarrassed about:	
1 Leaks and stains	42
2 Asking for pads or tampons in school	30
3 Carrying them in your bag	26
4 Swimming	22
5 Showers	12
6 Missing school	8
7 Teasing by boys	4
8 Teasing by girls	0
9 'Other things'	20

As can be seen from Table 4, three main anxieties were expressed by girls: 'leaks and stains', 'emergency supplies' and 'the problem of bags'. 'Swimming and showers' are explored later on in a discussion of lessons, particularly games, while 'anxieties about missing school' are considered separately.

'I leaked onto my school skirt and had to borrow my friend's coat'
High on the list of things that worried girls was the fear of 'leaking' while in school and getting blood on their clothes where it might be seen by others. This response was echoed in another section of the questionnaire where girls were asked to finish off a statement beginning 'The most embarrassing thing that could happen would be . . . .'. Here too girls felt that leaking generally would be acutely embarrassing, or, the ultimate horror story – onto a white skirt or trousers. These three examples relate to school:

> To leak all over my school skirt and not notice in a school lesson.

> The most embarrassing time was when I came on in RE and I leaked onto my school skirt and I didn't know, and was walking round in the classroom, so I had to borrow my friend's coat.

> To leak in games and be away from school and have to get back to change.

Another girl noted that her fear would be to have blood get on her *'outside* clothes'. This was something many other girls implied – with all the difficulties and associated worries this might bring, for example of body odour. As one girl said, 'I often just feel dirty all day until I can go, like, to a proper toilet and wash.'

Girls all worried about the practical arrangements of carrying round pads or tampons, which they often called 'stuff', in school, particularly when periods can be so irregular and often heavy. Their anxiety seemed to have two focus points: firstly an anxiety about being caught unawares in school and having to go to ask for emergency help, and second the difficulties of keeping 'stuff' privately but easily available in school bags or coat pockets, safe from the gaze of boys.

'She bangs it down so people know what it is'
Girls were most anxious about having to ask for emergency supplies in school, and perhaps the reasons for this anxiety will emerge more clearly when we look at the practical arrangements that exist in many schools. Several noted the difficulties involved in finding the school nurse at an appropriate time (if she was in school anyway) and of sometimes having to ask for help in the public setting of staff

room, corridor, or in the office of the school receptionist. As one girl said of the school nurse:

> She's kind but you have to go and find her, probably sitting there in the staff room with everybody else. Everybody looks at you and you have to say what you want. Lots of girls I know would sooner go to friends, so you go round half the school asking people you know. That can take up all the break.

And another says of going to the receptionist:

> Well there's often a queue there at break times and the office is full, so you have to wait like everybody else and just hope the boys will have gone. She isn't always nice about it and I think that she doesn't like having to do it herself. She kind of bangs it down so people know what it is, and you have to pay.

As in the example of leaking, there were many 'stories' of this kind, and girls referred to this kind of possibility even if it had not happened to them personally. It is a good example of how the 'dread' of something happening is almost as great a weight of responsibility as the actual event itself. Girls felt the need to be constantly vigilant in order to keep this event, as with so many other aspects of menstruation, at bay.

'If your bag got tipped out in class and everybody saw'
Over half of the girls felt that 'carrying stuff around' was also difficult. It is interesting that as they talked the nature of the difficulty emerged as being, retrospectively, worse in the past. The key problem in carrying 'things' or 'stuff' around seemed to be the fear of your school bag being upset or knocked over and pads or tampons being exposed in class. Sometimes this was not an accident, as one girl says:

> If you had pads in your bag and a boy was to tip your bag out and people saw them.

Although only four girls considered boys' behaviour of this kind to be a worry to them *now*, it was clear that in the past this had not been the case. For a younger age group – the second and third years in particular – some boys had seemed to reach a peak of teasing and vindictive harassment of girls in this way. Their teasing had involved crude language, touching girls as well as trying to expose them by deliberately emptying bags onto the floor. Not all such teasing behaviour had stopped however – for some girls reported that boys still did such things in the fourth year, although one feels that at this stage girls had more control over, and contempt for, boys' immaturity than previously. By fifteen to sixteen most girls seemed to have evolved a system for keeping pads or tampons wrapped up inside an inner pocket of school bags. They nevertheless vividly remembered experiences of boys tipping bags out, looking inside, throwing packets around the room or playing football with them. Out of school there were stories of boys doing similar things – kicking tampons onto the roof of the house for example, or slapping each other with a sanitary towel soaked in water. As we shall see below, difficulties also arose for girls in lessons, in how they took their bags to the loos to change, or extricated what they wanted from their bags without anybody seeing.

In all there were twenty extra comments in the space left for girls to add extra things to the list if they wished. They covered a wide range – concern about the effects of exercise and heavy bleeding (6 girls), the problems of leaking and odour (4 girls), notes and games, being asked questions in class (4 girls each) and about boys 'knowing'. In all then, forty of the fifty girls indicated that they were worried or embarrassed by at least two things related to practical effects of menstruation in school, half were anxious about three things, and no girl was entirely free of any worry at all.

As described these things relate to girls' feeling about how they personally might lose control either through an accident or through a deliberate act of provocation. In each case the anxiety or fear of embarrassment is about how to contain the private and personal nature of what is experienced and stop the fact of menstruation from being publicly exposed. A great deal of forethought and reflection seems to have gone into what must be therefore purely defensive and largely negative strategies of this kind.

(b) Practical arrangements: school facilities

Interview data suggested that most girls had experienced major problems in respect of school toilet and cloakroom facilities. I was relatively unprepared for the significance of this problem for girls, and so this aspect of things had not been explicitly explored in the questionnaire. However, many mentioned it when they were asked to complete a sentence starting 'The most difficult thing about having periods in school is . . .'. In all twenty-eight girls mentioned problems related to privacy and having to use school toilets at this time. For example:

> The toilets are always locked and when they are open there is never any tampax in the machines, so you have to ask at reception which is embarrassing.

> The lavatories are disgusting – wet and dirty and there's never soap or towels to wash your hands.

'You have to wedge the bin in front of the door'

Overall a number of features emerged from the interview and questionnaire in regard to school facilities. An important issue was graffiti and vandalization of lavatories and the consequences of this generally for all girls. A second and partly related issue was the availability of basic facilities in the toilets like soap or toilet paper, pads and tampons. A third was the extent to which toilets were open in school and where they were.

Many problems that girls described seemed to be the consequences of vandalism, although certainly not all. For example graffiti, whilst not actually damaging facilities, nevertheless led to closure of toilets because cleaners refused to go into them in that state. Toilet paper and paper towels were thrown around and stuffed down the toilets, so that they were blocked up and unpleasant to use.

One girl notes about privacy:

> You often have to wedge the bin in front of the door to stop it being pushed open. Sometimes it's the only one left at break so you have to use it or wait and be late.

> It was awful waiting around at break time until you thought the loos would be empty – you would spend all dinner time worrying about it and standing around.

There was often a partial or complete absence of toilet paper, soap and paper towels, and dispensing machines were often empty. In two schools there were no dispensing machines anyway, in one school they were rarely filled, and in a fourth there was no dispensing machine for tampons. Disposal facilities were frequently ill arranged, with disposal bins outside of the toilets, and in at least three accounts girls mentioned how difficult this had been for them when there were younger. Another girl noted about disposal:

> It's a kind of sick joke really, it's so embarrassing, we call it 'flush and run'.

Besides this, school toilets were often dirty and wet, and girls seemed not to know of any toilets that had washbasins inside that they could use in emergency in school time. One result of vandalism was that toilets were often locked in lesson time, with one left open near to an overlooked central place like reception. Other toilets might be closed completely because they were not cleaned or because of being repaired, so that those that were open in break time were more crowded and might be at some distance from far-flung classrooms. The cumulative consequences of all these factors for girls were varied. Some girls noted that they delayed visiting toilets at all in school whenever possible, preferring to 'nip out' to a local shopping centre or to go home at lunch time if they could. Some risked trouble by using the staff toilets which were quiet, clean and relatively private by comparison, but staff toilets were often locked or not easily approachable. The lack of facilities made changing towels or tampons unpleasant, unless girls took tissues from home, and proper hygiene difficult with no soap or method of drying their hands. One girl noted that she often got very sore in school because she wore two pads 'so that they would last all day', and others said that they only changed in school when absolutely necessary. The absence of dispensing machines meant that in an emergency a girl had to go off and seek help. This process might be lengthy because, as several girls noted, you went to the toilets first, then to find the school nurse or receptionist, waited until she was free and could be seen relatively privately, returned to the toilets and finally back to the lesson. Once back you might be asked by the class teacher to account for being late.

Overall the interviews particularly revealed a sense of many girls' disgust about school facilities, but in general a disgust that they had learned to put up with by the age of fifteen to sixteen. It was not always clear what their reactions had been at a younger age, but it seems safe to say that these would not have been more positive, and if anything that they probably felt worse at this stage.

So far the consequences and implications for girls of menstruation and the school setting have been explored in terms of embarrassment, fears and anxieties, and the practical environment of school toilet and cloakroom facilities. Now we look at some of the things that girls have to say about being in the classroom generally and specific lessons.

(c) Being in lessons: games and talking to teachers

Of all lessons it was games lessons that served as the focus for most anxieties in girls' comments. Over thirty girls specifically mentioned showers or swimming as something that caused worry or embarrassment and another fourteen girls spontaneously brought up games in open-ended questions in the questionnaire. In the most direct and obvious sense games make problems for girls because they raise physical difficulties that must be overcome or explained, and because explaining or subsequent absence from an activity may be noticed by others. Swimming and showers are possibly the most obvious manifestations of girls' difficulties in this regard and, from what they said, figure large in early schooling as issues of embarrassment and anxiety. As one girl said:

> The most difficult thing is when you have to be excused from swimming and the teacher starts questioning you.

'He said "speak up, I can't hear you" '

Later, however, physical exercise and associated problems of pain or feeling unwell and 'leaking' are more important. How teachers dealt with girls' explanations and excuses was an added aspect to this anxiety. In many schools now games are taught to boys and girls by male and female teachers and many sports are done in mixed groups. The possibilities therefore for exposure of a girl's 'state' to male members of staff and boys is vastly increased – something that girls seemed to dread. This makes sense if we remembered who girls felt that they could and could not talk to about menstruation in school. In general anyway, but particularly for girls, there appears to be an atmosphere of disbelief and an assumption of 'skiving' around not doing games. Girls who took notes were not automatically believed:

> I took my note up to him, and he didn't even open it. There were others there and he said, 'Well why can't you do games, tell me.' So I muttered and looked embarrassed and he said, 'Speak up, I can't hear you.' Then he said, 'Well that's no excuse. I thought women these days had all *that* under control.'

The girl in question did not know whether she had been excused or not so she waited until she could see the games teacher alone. He told her to go and speak to a woman games teacher and 'get it sorted out' because 'there was no excuse to miss games these days'. In fact she had very heavy periods and could not do any activity, 'even coughing or blowing my nose', without losing blood. Several other girls wrote on the questionnaire that they worried about such things, and also about doing games whilst feeling ill or with stomach cramps. However, not all male teachers were unsympathetic, and not all unsympathetic games teachers were male; in some cases women games teachers had been equally dismissive:

> She kept saying, 'It's just natural, there's nothing to worry about. The exercise will do you good, it's laziness,' and made me go out. I had to sit down in the cold most of the time because I felt so bad.

And, a factor that is often forgotten, girls themselves frequently did actually *want* to do games – at least eight girls seemed to be indicating that they missed games activities that they enjoyed:

> It's horrible because you miss trampolining.

> I enjoy swimming usually but sometimes I can't.

The argument that periods are 'natural' and therefore somehow without serious consequences was one frequently used by teachers, as was the injunction that 'exercise is good for period pains'. Being fit and taking exercise is supposed to be generally good for menstrual problems, but asking some girls to do hectic exercise when they are bleeding heavily or feeling bad and away from home, and to treat them inconsiderately when they prefer not to, does not seem helpful. It is not clear whether girls understood arguments about 'naturalness' and how 'exercise' helped: to them it felt like patronizing disbelief.

'I think teachers should be more understanding'

Girls also worried about things in lessons more generally – they found the issue of taking bags to the cloakroom whilst in lesson difficult, and also coping with questions about the need to visit toilets in the middle of lessons, or being late. This embarrassment was not helped by boys who might keep an observant eye on girls' activities and lose no opportunity for teasing. As one girl noted:

> If you take your bag out with you they say, 'We know why you did that,' and you feel really silly doing it.

On the other hand removing packets from your bag in class has other embarrassing possibilities:

I took them out and put them up my jumper, but the teacher saw me and said, 'What have you got up there?'

I was rushing out and they fell onto the floor in the front of the class.

Girls dreaded most of all the possibility that they might stain their clothes in class without knowing, as has been described earlier. Like ' "stuff" dropping out of your bag' and 'having to tell a teacher in public', 'leaking' was a major dread and figured powerfully in girls' stories, even though it might never happen to them (although it did to at least one girl in the sample). But obtaining permission to go to the toilet in lesson time, in order to forestall this dread, was not always simple because sometimes teachers questioned girls about going. For example, ten girls noted things like:

Changing during the lesson without the teacher asking you a question and making it obvious to the boys why you are going to the toilet.

Having to put up with immature boys and being questioned by the teacher.

I think that teachers should be more understanding and allow girls to go to the toilet when you need to change, without being questioned. It would save a lot of embarrassment.

However, girls were not entirely without resources and responses, as other 'stories' illustrate:

I wanted to go to the loos desperately in the lesson time and he said 'Why now? Just wait till this bit's done and go later.' So I said, 'I can't,' and he said 'Why?' So I said, 'Because of women's problems,' and he was so embarrassed.

And another 'story' that caused hysterical laughter from the group where it was told:

It was the deputy head, and there was this girl called Smiley, who weren't scared of nobody. And she asked to go out, and he was all bad tempered as usual and said 'No'. She asked again and he said 'No', so she shouted out, really loud – *'I've got my period, Sir.'*

(d) Feeling ill: missing school or 'sitting at the back'

It would seem from accounts of actual experiences, as well as 'stories', that the experience of menstruation in school could be fraught with anxiety for some girls. If to this we add the evidence about how they are feeling at this time in terms of symptoms it would perhaps not be surprising if girls coped by taking time off. What then did girls say about managing feeling ill in school?

First it is interesting to note that few girls did take time off school on a regular basis. Almost half of the sample 'never took time off' and eighteen girls noted taking 'odd days off'. However, two girls took up to a day off regularly, while eight regularly took more than a day off.

'They just say it's natural'

Almost all girls had devised strategies for coping in school, mostly ad hoc and personal. Although 'pain' was the most obvious symptom, girls felt there was little to be done. Few girls mentioned any more treatments than aspirin, rest or hot water bottles for period pains, while emotional symptoms seemed mysterious in origin and treatment. As a girl said:

> Sometimes I can stop the pain, but I can never stop feeling depressed and moody. It just comes over me and I look fat and horrible and have spots. It just all gets me down but I can never stop it even though everybody knows it's coming . . .

Others had been to the doctor, for example:

> I get pain for two days. He says it's natural and can't give you anything really.

Or avoided the doctor:

> I wanted to go, but my Mum said he would only give me the pill, so I didn't go.

Many schools do not supply aspirin (so girls would have to bring their own or find alternative supplies) and hot water bottles and rest are not possible unless girls go to the rest room and lie down. Most girls chose to manage in class by sitting still and quietly at the back unless they were feeling very ill indeed. Many girls discussed 'managing' in this way in the interviews.

> You kind of sit there trying not to let anybody see you are feeling bad, sort of bent over and holding yourself to stop the pain.

> You can't really move – it's murder moving from lesson to lesson.

> Kind of all crouched up because of pains in the lower part of my stomach.

And to remind readers of a powerful quote used earlier:

While you have pains in your stomach and head and everywhere else you have teachers telling you what to do – to behave and get on with your work. They don't know what is happening and how you feel. I find it hard to sit down and actually concentrate on my work. One day I spent a whole day trying to concentrate which was impossible. I wish teachers could actually sense you are not well so they could be more sympathetic.

'If their periods are OK, they think ours are too'

Others mentioned sitting over or against radiators as a source of heat, or 'trying to concentrate hard to get interested so you might forget it'. A few girls said that they had been to see the school nurse, if she had been there, and she had been generally kind and helpful. However, many girls did not wish to miss lessons conspicuously, by defining themselves as *really ill* – ill enough to go and lie down or to go home. Perhaps they did not wish to be seen as ill *because of periods*. Most girls managed both physical and emotional symptoms by 'shutting down', keeping quiet and still and getting by until they felt a bit better. As girls got older they obviously got wiser too – for example, problems about games had been solved by avoiding games altogether, in the many ways that pupils learn as they go through school:

> I always do volunteer work so that I can make an excuse without a note now – haven't done games for years!

For most girls saying anything was out of the question, particularly to male teachers, and women teachers were not *necessarily* seen as more sympathetic generally, as one girl said:

> Every period I get really ill and no one seems to understand. Female teachers aren't very understanding because if their periods are OK they think ours are too. *But no one is the same!*

Finally it is interesting to note that although several girls had experienced problems with mocks or end-of-year exams, none had wondered how they would manage, or what they would or could do in the future if their periods came at that time. They were surprised and a little thrown by my question: nobody had ever mentioned this issue in school and they seemed to feel that there was nothing anybody could do anyway. Girls were not offered and did not expect any help. Coping with exams, like other aspects of schooling, was something that girls had to bear, to overcome at a private and individual level – part of the 'normal and natural process' of being a girl and having periods in school.

Summary and discussion

In summary then, it is clear that many girls were experiencing physical and emotional symptoms of menstruation as they got older, and that by sixteen many were feeling off colour, unwell or in some cases quite ill, regularly each month. Many described how the combination of physical and emotional symptoms was particularly upsetting, in that their ability to cope was thereby lessened, and also how the physical effects themselves made them feel 'fed up'. Most girls experienced aspects of what is commonly called the social taboos around menstruation in relation to talking about it, fear of exposure, teasing and ridicule and feeling 'ashamed' and embarrassed. They felt these aspects both as external social pressure and also from within themselves – the potential of menstruation as a secret thing in their own minds, thoughts and actions. Nevertheless all girls had someone whom they felt they could talk to openly and ask about problems, mostly friends and mothers, and in school some women teachers or the school nurse. Many studies of menstruation, particularly those done in the USA (see Grief and Ulman 1982), have explored these relationships and contacts as a major source of informational and emotional learning – the young woman receiving ideas that shape her attitude to periods both from significant others and from the atmosphere of 'taboo' that surrounds them.

However, such studies do not take into account the social and material context of the setting where girls have to spend much of their lives. Although these may be various, most girls would seem to be based in two key locations for much of this time: home and school.

This is not to deny the influence of media, friends and girls' social lives, but to suggest that home and school provide a structured situation within which having periods must be dealt with in a practical sense. These practicalities and practices thus set the scene for and provide girls with their first lived experience, a model of how menstruation may be socially valued and provided for as a real thing, in the world outside of home and school. Nevertheless school is different from home in major respects. At home a girl can cope in relative privacy, and she may, if she is lucky, have sympathetic female (or male) support. This division between home and school may offer girls their first experience of demarcation between the private and public realms, a demarcation that runs through so much of women's personal, family and reproductive lives as they get older. Whatever the home provides, girls still have to learn to manage periods alone in the public world outside. Later many women will encounter this split again at work, an experience that may extend to include the practical consequences of pregnancy and motherhood as they are embodied in work practices, and rights and obligations.

As girls described it, the arrangements offered in school often made their lives more difficult, not less. Clearly some school facilities were vandalized by girls themselves (although it was suggested in one school that boys also broke into the girls' toilets) but the extent to which the actions of a few girls are allowed to change school policy and provision is an important issue, and other solutions seem possible that do not penalize girls generally in such an unpleasant fashion. 'Vandalism' should not be allowed to disguise the fact that facilities in school anyway are either bad or totally absent, and that provision for girls pays little regard to their feelings and experiences, to say the least. Girls learned avoidance tactics, how to use other more pleasant facilities, how to hide things in their bags or coat pockets, and to 'manage' teasing. Some girls had developed a quick humour that turned the latent embarrassment of 'periods' to their own account. Overall however, the interviews left a sense of the disgust that many girls had learned for the whole process of coping in school, and resentment that it took up so much energy and time to get by. However, even if girls did 'cope', much of this time was 'negative' time – spent keeping things invisible – not doing positive and helpful things for themselves. Above all, girls seemed to spend a great deal of time 'dreading' that something might happen – the subject of many stories – a powerful indicator of how 'negativity' operated more widely to structure girls' thoughts and behaviour. 'Leaking in public', 'dropping your stuff' or 'having to tell a male teacher' were the mythic frameworks to this dread, which often came to a head in games lessons. Girls were asked (or told) to do games in revealing clothes, with few basic facilities, because exercise is good for period pains! Not surprisingly some girls learned how to avoid games, and perhaps many learned to view games as unpleasant and anxiety provoking. In seeing such girls as reluctant or skiving it is possible that we seriously underestimate the numbers of girls who *want* to do games, and the longer-term problem of women's exercise, fitness and health is also at stake here, in that the negative lessons of school may shape future attitudes. It is deeply ironic that girls are urged to do games in a fashion that may ultimately destroy the possibility both of their enjoyment and of helping the very problem that underlies their resistance in the first place.

The full consequences of these aspects of girls' experience in school are unknown. Girls preferred to hide their difficulties and struggle along as usual, finding individual solutions, talking to close friends or a friendly teacher (if there is one). Girls sat at the back, kept quiet, tried to concentrate and generally 'got by'. Most were resigned that nothing could be done to help them anyway, beyond rest, a hot water bottle or an aspirin. What girls valued above all, it seemed, was a sympathetic and responsible sharing of the difficulties, an understanding, particularly in respect of feeling upset and depressed. This did not necessarily mean that girls wanted to miss school, indeed most did not anyway, unless things got very bad. Schools appear to have no mechanism that accepts menstruation at a public level; as elsewhere this means that women's needs are largely ignored – and institutionally invisible. In this respect it is interesting to compare girls' experience in school with the coping mechanisms evolved by adult women, and to chart how extensive, pervasive and automatic such coping mechanisms become, as women seek to mitigate and control the effects periods may have on their lives. This is in part possible because the menstrual cycle may be more predictable and symptoms less acute for adult women, and also because the context is more in their control. Planning ahead, slowing down, and rearranging work may be possible strategies, as well as more practical things like taking the pill and using tampons. Women are more likely to demand proper facilities and basic privacy, and to challenge men, if teasing or unpleasant comments are made, from a basis of experience or collective solidarity. Few of these possibilities are available to girls in school, even if they gained the confidence to state their needs. Most girls try to manage and to say nothing – coping with the facilities the school provides and surviving the day-to-day difficulties as best they can. Thus periods are made invisible. If girls have problems then they have to speak and make them public, yet in itself this is difficult. Girls who do speak out are quite likely to be met by the stock school position – that periods are 'normal and natural', to make them public is to make a fuss or ask for special treatment. In fact nothing could be further from the truth, and many of the difficulties that girls experience are a direct result of this double standard.

Although both girls and adult women suffer generally from such a double standard, as Sophie Laws notes:

> Hiding the existence of periods forces women to be endlessly aware of men's potential presence, their gaze entering even the most private and mundane parts of a woman's life. And, if women do not speak in public about periods, they are blocked from generating new understandings of their bodies which would challenge such views. (1985, p. 29)

I would argue that school represents, in its degree of closedness and control, a particularly harsh learning environment not repeated to the same extent in the everyday world out of school. For girls, as they 'grow up', no lesson could be more painfully learned.

Acknowledgements

Thanks are due to the schools, the teachers and pupils who took part in the pilot study, in 1987, which provided the impetus for this paper.

Bibliography and further reading

Allen, I. (1987) 'Education in Sex and Personal Relationships', PSI Research Report 665, Oxford PSI.

Chandler, E. (1980) *Educating Adolescent Girls*, Unwin Educational Books.

The Clarity Collective (1983) *Taught not Caught Strategies for Sex Education*, Learning Dev. Aids, Wisbech, Cambridgeshire.

Goldman and Goldman (1982) *Children's Sexual Knowledge*, Routledge and Kegan Paul.

Grief, E. B. and Ulman, K. J. (1982) 'The Psychological Impact of Menarche on Early Adolescent Females: A review of the literature', *Child Development*, Vol. 53, No. 6, Dec.

Laws, S., Hey, V., Eagan, V. (1985) *Seeing Red: The politics of premenstrual tension*, Hutchinson.

Laws, S. (1985) 'Male Power and Menstrual Etiquette', in H. Homans (ed.) *The Sexual Politics of Reproduction*, Gower.

Lee, C. (1983) *The Ostrich Position. Sex Schooling and Mystification*, Writers and Readers.

McFadyean, M. (1986) Youth in Distress: Letters to Just Seventeen, *Health Education Journal*, Vol. 45, No. 1.

Measor, L. and Woods, P. (1984) *Changing Schools: Pupils' Perspectives on Transfer to a Comprehensive*, Milton Keynes, Open University Press.
Weideger, P. (1977) *Female Cycles*, The Women's Press.
Went, D. (1985) *Sex Education, Some Guideline for Teachers*, Bell and Hyman.

CHAPTER 8

Trying Not Just to Survive: A Lesbian Teacher in a Boys' School

ISOBEL GILL

In 1986 Isobel Gill published an article in *Teaching London Kids*, a journal for teachers in London. Called 'Miss is a Lesbian', it described Isobel's experiences as a white lesbian teacher in a boys' secondary school. In this chapter part of this article is reprinted, after which Isobel describes how some of these earlier ideas formed the basis of the document which she produced for the school suggesting anti-sexist, anti-heterosexist initiatives.

1. Extract from 'Miss is a Lesbian': March 1986

A paradoxical position

A lesbian feminist teaching boys is in a paradoxical position. My approach is not to try to identify the 'gay' student in each of my groups and to give him some special attention. I want to engage all the students in becoming aware of, and examining, the conditioning process which damages all of us, which conditions us towards accepting heterosexuality as 'the real world'. In journeying to find out why homosexual experience and politics is seen as aberrant, a student, a colleague will have to think carefully through his/her own experience and ask – What world is challenged by homosexual experience? What world does a radical gay politics envision? Where do I stand in relation to this? It is easy enough to plan a radical curriculum and see that books and classroom materials need replacing. What is difficult is to imagine how this radical curriculum could adhere in the ideological ground occupied by schools at the moment.

Every day the lesbian and gay teacher is involved in making a different ground – a meeting point between his/her experience and the homophobic attitudes expressed by the school – students and teachers. S/he needs this ground to walk on – it is not just an ideological exercise but a necessary condition for survival.

Each day the white male gay teacher in this school runs the gauntlet of a barrage of insult – 'AIDS victim', 'battyman', 'bender'. If he is known to be gay, boys may well run round the room clutching their bottoms and refuse to come to detentions in case he 'jumps on' them. . . . In a vulnerable position anything can be picked on. And wearing skirts won't help. Being assertive in the classroom, refusing to be flirted with, challenging any sexist or heterosexist comments, I am still described as 'being like a man'. As a lesbian teacher I am also taunted by the images of so-called 'lesbian behaviour' which the boys (and the staff?) have culled from pornographic videos and magazines. 'Dirty lesbian', 'Greenham lesbian' shouted out of the window, screamed down the corridor, pornographic scratchings on desk tops and walls leave no room for dialogue. 'Miss is a lesbian' is written on my door. 'So what' I write beneath. I go on existing, I go on teaching my lessons. Maybe on some days the atmosphere is soft enough, I have enough energy to take an insult into a conversation, to 'talk it through' with a student, to re-interpret physically threatening behaviour as a quest for information.

However it is very rare that the current of homophobia lessens enough for this creative point to be explored by the teacher and student(s) at the same time. This is the common ground I'm talking about.

The 'out' male gay teacher, the lesbian, walks the school as – at best – an advertisement, but always more objectified, 'larger than life', than the heterosexual teacher. S/he experiences 'acceptance' or rejection – but the solid block of authority which makes these decisions needs shifting, is sure of its right to judge, doesn't want to shift.

Whose problem?

How do other members of staff react? In the case of the white gay male teacher in this predominantly male staffroom, circles which pride themselves on being progressive see him as a 'mascot', an opportunity to show their liberalism – and even a person with whom to flirt – to try out a pose or a stance, a 'little patch for their wildness to grow in'. 'Gary's all right. He's a poof.' When a white gay male teacher in a relatively high position in the hierarchy chose to bring his harassment to the attention of the powers that be – in order perhaps to test out their attitudes/politics/procedure – what happened was that the 'problem' was personalized, it was for the gay teacher to deal with, after all, hadn't he brought it upon himself by being visible? Is it this same analysis which prevents any information supporting or acknowledging young gay experience from being pinned up in the sixth-form room? And when the school's gay teacher group gave support to a sixth-form boy who had begun to identify as gay they were attacked as encouraging him. An 'out' gay teacher acts as a lifeline to students struggling with their feelings, but this help is seen by the authority as subversive. Because these feelings are not celebrated, but seen as troublesome and dangerous, the support we can give is pushed into limited, and at times furtive, channels. Nor am I referring to the few students who call themselves gay before they leave school. Gay and lesbian teachers are 'used' in many ways – a student's quest for talk and information about sensual feelings may well be focused on the gay teacher who is perceived as a sexual being; whether he or she welcomes that perception or not.

As a white lesbian in a boys' school I am in an even more vulnerable position than my white gay male colleagues. How can I trust the hierarchy to support me when I share with that hierarchy no common language or experience? If men are not the centre of my world, then why am I coming to them for help? I am likely to cause them trouble, to make them uncomfortable. Is it any wonder that lesbians and gay men put in so much time and energy on Anti-Sexist Initiatives, Equal Opportunities Policies, Gender Issues – who else shares our urgency?

Despite my commitment to working in these areas, I still feel some disquiet; resentment at always being looked to as an authority on 'sexual politics' (I think my position as a keeper of other people's consciences can only mean I do most of the work), and anger, that as a lesbian who has her own share of internalized homophobia, I put precious energy into starting a women's group – and then felt I could not use this group to support me in my specific harassment as a lesbian – in case it frightened off the women who had already found it difficult to come to a 'women only' meeting. In any school-based group meeting around anti-sexist, anti-racist issues I worry in case opening my mouth will discredit the very cause I am supporting. 'Of course she is bound to speak up' – and of course I do.

. . . And now I feel like saying to my heterosexual colleagues, 'you tell me what's urgent for you – if you don't show your rejection of mainstream attitudes about relating, then you are colluding with them'. It is always the burden of the homosexual teacher to identify and explain and point to all solutions.

2. Reflections: March 1987

So, having re-read the article, I ask myself in March 1987: What has
been possible and what is possible? The article itself was read and
discussed seriously (if covertly) by friends in the staff room and has
a 'life beyond' – being used in the anti-heterosexism course run for
PGCE students at the Institute of Education, London University.

The article was written before the school was struck by the full
force of AIDS hysteria. At its height a boy only had to sneeze in class
to prompt cries of 'AIDS victim'. That refrain was thrown at gay
male colleagues, from windows, or as boys backed away from them
down corridors. A great deal of shoe leather was worn out chasing
those who shouted. And it was all horrifying and depressing. It
seemed that any ground which had been made clear to present
homosexual experience in, for example a 'Personal Relationships'
course, had been swept away. 'Gay' had become synonymous in the
boys' minds with 'infected' – and the effect of the gutter press was to
encourage suggestions that all homosexuals should be put on an
island and blown up. Our efforts to inform the students were quick,
informal, ad hoc. We placed Terence Higgins Trust leaflets in all the
staff's pigeon-holes so that the burden for re-education could be
shared. Those who were most threatened by the new ferocity in the
atmosphere organized this initiative – the effect was not monitored.
It seems safer for the 'Authorities' that anti-heterosexist education
proceeds in this informal manner.

And the hysteria died down. We organized a lunchtime book
display of lesbian and gay writing for adults and children which
many colleagues explored with interest. A copy of *Jenny Lives with
Eric and Martin* (Bosche 1983) (before the media furore) received no
less and no more attention than any other of the books for children.

Now, a year later, many of the students know how to spell 'condom'. The recent spate of television programmes on AIDS-related
illness has meant that a vocabulary for sexuality has begun to be
used publicly and the kids have begun to learn a little more about
sexual behaviour. Gay men have appeared on the screen to be
likeable and reasonable people. This is all helpful to those of us on
the rock-face who have previously produced the climate and content for discussion from our own selves, our lives.

In school, the materiography 'Positive Images' prepared and dis-
tributed by the ILEA suddenly confirmed our existence. It lists
plays, stories, videos and articles by and about lesbians and gay

men. This materiography is a tremendous help – a proof that such work, such a culture and community of lesbians and gay men exists, and also an incentive to explore the work described within. The existence of the document assumes that there are interested parties 'out there' who wish to take part in the liberating task of anti-heterosexist education – and that not all of these people will already define themselves as gay or lesbian. The materiography is a contribution to developing curriculum – and this is an important step to take, since it moves us on from the 'lesbian and gay issue' being seen *only* as about employment rights, towards something to do with education – for all.

3. The document

Then the ILEA asked schools to produce an equal opportunities document relating to gender issues; and after our years of working out a grass-roots consciousness-raising to achieve a climate in which such a document could appear in our school, the opportunity had to be grasped. Were it not for those early years, for the people, several of whom have now left, who provided the momentum for such a document, this task would have been impossible. We have seen our women's group struggle on (despite a senior member of staff who sees its existence as divisive), the mixed anti-sexist consciousness-raising group come and go.

I had the responsibility for preparing the document and a small amount of time was given for this task. This quickly ran out so I took the document home, hunting in existing policies for help. ILEA's 'Anti-sexist statement' shows awareness of both the impoverishment of 'sex-stereotyping' and the operation of sexism in girls' and women's lives. (I lifted two paragraphs from this document.) Nowhere are the words 'lesbian' or 'gay' used, nor is the existence of institutional heterosexism recognized. The all-important sentence reads: 'The ILEA is committed to achieving an education which provides capacity of opportunity and freedom from discrimination on grounds of race, sex, class, sexuality or disability in both education and employment.' That word 'sexuality' is the nod in the direction of my existence and for that I am grateful.

To call our document 'anti-sexist and anti-heterosexist' was a step away from the blandness of 'equal opportunities' and 'gender'. I found the task of writing a policy document very difficult. I tried to see it as a pragmatic task, a kind of writing no one reads, but at the same time I felt exposed; that I was constructing both an explanation and a defence.

The days of the GLC provided me with two precious books: 'Changing the World' – a charter for lesbian and gay rights – and 'Danger: Heterosexism at Work' – an analysis of heterosexism in the workplace. The English Centre (Ebury Street) book on gender issues for English teachers was also helpful, as were the papers which had come out of our school's Women's Group – particularly those on how to respond to students in cases of our being sexually harassed. I read pamphlets such as 'Haringey Black Gays and Lesbians Speak Out', and the correspondence in ILEA's newspaper *Contact* – letters to educate that being gay or lesbian was not an immoral stance in the world. A new anthology of black gay writing from the States, *In the Life* (Beam 1986), was invaluable to my preparation. (In it I found also a poem called 'When I stopped kissing my father' which I want my lower-school classes to read.)

But in the end I put all these books and articles away and returned to familiar sources – particularly a chapter called 'Compulsory Heterosexuality and Lesbian Existence' in 'On Lies, Secrets and Silence' by Adrienne Rich.

> To take the step of questioning heterosexuality as a 'preference' or 'choice' for women – and to do the intellectual and emotional work that follows – will call for a special quality of courage in heterosexually identified feminists but I think the rewards will be great: A freeing-up of thinking, the exploring of new paths, the shattering of another great silence, new clarity in personal relationships.
>
> (Rich 1980)

It took me a while to realize that the task was difficult because I had to keep calling to mind distress, squeeze the feelings out and translate the experience into a moral imperative, an educational practice. In the middle of all this it was an upset fourth year who gave me help, by writing about what he was suffering:

> Some of the kids call me a poof because of the way my words come out. It's not my fault and when they start to all join in I feel like punching one of them straight in the face and showing them up, but in the end I know that it is wrong to stir trouble so I calm down. They don't seem to like the way I dress or the way I style my hair. I think that people owe me more than this. It would be good to know what the real life is.

I think our talking together gave him support, but as the day for the document to be discussed drew nearer it was my own sense of 'real life' which I felt under threat. Fantasies of the meeting plagued me and my gay male colleague; that we would be denounced by even those nearest to us, a heroic statement of our right to exist would have to be made, followed by an exit from the room. For several days I travelled with a private library of writing which would quash the attacks I imagined would inevitably come. And I know the final words of 'Hard Words: Why lesbians have to be philosophers' by Sheila Shulman by heart. These I kept repeating to myself:

> Either the world is going to move over
> and make plenty of room for me
> or it's going to choke on me but
> it's not going to spit me out
>
> they say to me on behalf of the world
> but there is plenty of room
> their generosity is presumptuous
> no one speaks to me on behalf of the world
> I am the world as they are
> indigenous wildlife see like trees
> and dolphins and children
> as innocent as natural and perhaps
> though I'm sure they can hardly stomach the thought
> more human because necessarily
> more conscious
> think about that for awhile

(from *One Foot on the Mountain*, Mokin 1979)

In the event, the meeting was postponed. The following week we gathered again. A senior member of staff had asked that we produce a cover sheet of terms and was anxious that 'heterosexual' was not synonymous with 'heterosexist'. There were no denunciations (except from an evangelical Christian) but the meeting ran out of time to discuss the paper after a member of senior management spoke for twenty-five minutes against the existence of the Women's Group.

So much for our efforts. So much for the messages of support from former students (gay) pledging their willingness to talk to staff and parents on how this document would have made a difference to their school lives.

As I write, the chances for the document being discussed again are very slight. The school is faced with amalgamation. One-third of the staff have been issued with redeployment notices. Tomorrow we go on strike against the Baker Bill.[1] What price equal opportunities statements when those who have worked and shared ideas over many years are being split up, dispersed; the climate in which these ideas can flourish vanishing with these people?

Here is the document. I wish it luck.

4. Anti-sexism and anti-heterosexism – a draft document

I. *Sexism and heterosexism: introducing the terms*

We live in a society whose institutions and dominant ideology maintain the idea of male superiority through sexist practices. It is also a society which uses heterosexist practices, supporting the idea that only heterosexual experience is 'normal' or 'natural'. The school community has a responsibility to challenge such false definitions of what it is to be a man or a woman in the world and must work to diminish the suffering caused by sexism and heterosexism.

II. *Sexism: its effect upon women in general*

Although men and women are *all* trying to define themselves despite the limits society places on them because of their gender, it is women and girls who suffer most in society from the effects of sexism. Greater value and status is given to traditionally male pursuits and occupations than to traditionally female ones. This generally places men in positions of power over women, whether at home, at work, or through the political, social and economic systems and institutions which govern our lives. Only some of the more obvious forms of discrimination women suffer have been made illegal by the Sex Discrimination and Equal Pay Acts.

III. *Sexism: its effect upon women in school*

We have all been affected by the conditioning of society, and it is hardly surprising that sexist and heterosexist attitudes are so deeply ingrained and so easily expressed by the students en masse. These views are transmitted and reinforced not only by the media, but also in the organization of schools. In general men predominate in decision-making posts and subject areas such as Science where the status is greater and where the subject matter is considered to be a rational body of knowledge associated with abstract thought. School caretakers are generally male; cleaners, helpers and secretaries almost exclusively female, and less well paid. Boys too easily feel that a woman member of staff being assertive is for her to step out of line, and that she can be legitimately abused because she does not conform to what they have been taught is a woman's work or place.

We welcome the appointment of women to positions of authority in this school believing that this will implicitly support women workers who are daily challenging sexist attitudes and male superiority. It will also help those who do not rely upon traditional male forms of control and authority to secure happy relationships between boys and staff.

IV.   Sexual harassment of women within the school community

We all have the basic human right to work in an atmosphere which is not threatening nor professionally limiting, and in which we feel our contributions as workers are valued. Within the school community it is clear that there are those who do not believe that all share in that right. Women staff suffer daily sexual harassment through words and gestures, through graffiti and other forms of behaviour designed to remind them of their role as the subordinates and servicers of men.

This sexual abuse and intimidation is a commonplace women's experience, but it is not inevitable that it should continue. All members of this school affirm that no one should have to suffer these expressions of sexism and that we all have a responsibility to develop strategies to stop this behaviour as well as to understand why it is so endemic.

V.   Sexual harassment of lesbians and gay males within the school community

In economic and social life, gay men and lesbians of all ages face prejudice and discrimination. This 'homophobia' means that they are denied full access to health care, and are discriminated against in employment and in housing. They suffer from the threat or from the fact of having their children taken away from them. They often suffer alienation from their own families.

A heterosexist society, that is, a society which promotes and rewards the idea that only heterosexuality and heterosexual family life is 'normal' or 'natural', stifles any information to the contrary and seeks to punish lesbians and gay men for questioning its assumptions about 'normality'. Lesbian and gay staff suffer daily sexual harassment at school as a result of these unconsciously held attitudes – through words such as 'poof', 'queer', 'batty man' or 'lezzie', through gestures and behaviour intended to tell gay men or lesbians that they are 'unnatural', inferior, disgusting, infected, and that their right to exist depends only upon the goodwill of the heterosexual ('real') world. At the same time they are accused of being predators and seducers of youth.

All members of this school affirm that no one should have to suffer these expressions of heterosexism, and affirm their commitment to challenge them when they occur as well as understand why they occur.

VI.   Harassment of those who do not conform to sexual stereotypes

Those male members of staff who do not rely on unquestioning notions of male identity and superiority to give themselves protection and validity, and boys who do not seem to conform in appearance and manner to current stereotypes of what it is to be male, can also suffer physical and verbal harassment. Such individuals must be supported against the conditioning of society which threatens to push them back towards narrow and destructive views of themselves and their place in the world.

VII.   The need for resources for re-education

All such harassment must be challenged. In order to do this constructively and intelligently, many ingrained fears and prejudices within ourselves may have to be re-examined and fought. We must all ask ourselves how and why our own sexuality is formed.

Staff and students who are working to deepen their understanding of the issues raised by this anti-sexist and anti-heterosexist initiative need access to relevant books, articles, resource packs, films, videos, courses and groups. They also need access to those who are already working in these areas, such as Women's Theatre Groups or the Lesbian and Gay Black Group, and so on. The whole staff supports the existence of those in our own school who have a special and informed contribution to make to these issues (such as the women's group and the gay teachers group) and welcomes the opportunity to learn from the experiences and strategies these groups may be willing to share. A primary aim of this is to demonstrate that all staff and students are of equal value.

VIII. Checking out materials

Sexism and heterosexism thrive on myths, fears and prejudices. In the materials we use in all subject areas in the classroom we must check that stereotypical views of women and men, of lesbians and gay men are not being used in an uncritical way. We must also celebrate and make visible the achievements of women, lesbians and gay men as well as those of heterosexual men. If our students are to be independent learners they must be helped to be able to detect bias and prejudice in materials they encounter in school and outside. Our methods in the classroom should encourage co-operative and collaborative work rather than competition.

IX. Reconsidering the language of control

We must also check that we are not contributing to the degrading of women, lesbians and gay men by being thoughtless in our language, for example, by saying to boys that they are behaving like 'a lot of silly girls', or that boys who are fighting should 'stop cuddling one another'. In these cases order has been restored at the expense of men who wish to show their affection for each other. Authoritarian tactics towards the boys in the classroom and an 'all boys together' attitude outside the classroom need to be examined. We must consider to what extent this 'world of boys and men' thrives at the expense of truth about the lives and experiences of women, gay men and lesbians, and limits those men who consider themselves to be heterosexual.

X. Peer pressure and the stereotype trap

Boys who do not conform to the sexist stereotypes taught to and held by their peers endure great suffering at school and they have a right to expect support for their struggles. We must challenge the way boys harass each other physically or by sexist and homophobic abuse, as well as understanding and explaining why this aggression is such a common part of boys' life. We must create situations and the emotional climate in which boys' real experiences and softer feelings can be shared without risking loss of face, loss of friends, charges of being 'queer' and physical harassment. Students have the right to learn about men in a variety of roles, expressing a wide range of emotions and living in differing life-styles and relationships counter to gender stereotypes.

XI.   Changing the curriculum

Students should also be given the opportunity to develop a socio-logical and historical understanding of the nature of sexism and heterosexism. They have a right to know why the truths of women's lives have been kept hidden or altered to conform to male sexist stereotypes, and why there are such levels of hatred and ignorance about the experiences of lesbians and gay men. They have a right to know about the effects of that hatred (for example, one in five teenagers interviewed in a research project carried out by the Gay Teenage Group had made a suicide attempt because of heterosexist pressure). We must also check that the subject choices offered to students are not stereotypically gender-based, thus limiting career choices and experiences.

XII.   Parents' involvement

Parents must be given enough encouragement and opportunity to express their experiences of sexism, and should expect support from staff in challenging those attitudes outside school. Lesbian and gay parents' experiences and contributions are also to be welcomed and respected. All parents should feel able to complain about the effects of sexism and heterosexism on their children in expectation of sup-port from the school for their distress and action to diminish its source.

N.B.   Some definitions

Heterosexism: a system of ideas and practices based on a set of beliefs about heterosexuality being the normal and natural sexuality for both women and men, and all other sexual practices, in particu-lar homosexuality, being deviant. Heterosexism lays down the rules and conditions under which all sexualities are valued or devalued in our society, and penalties/benefits accordingly awarded. Under heterosexism, lesbians and gay men are particularly penalized.

Sexism: prejudice or adverse discrimination on the basis of either a person's sex or stereotypical views of masculine and feminine roles.

Homophobia: fear of relationships with the same sex, or fear of loving the same sex, and fear and loathing of those who do love the same sex.

Throughout this policy document the use of the words 'lesbian', 'gay' and 'homosexual' shall include those who choose to define themselves as bi-sexual and anyone who chooses to express or acknowledge the homosexual part of themselves.

This document assumes that many people who define themselves as heterosexual do not subscribe to heterosexist ideas or practices.

Note

1 Education Act 1987.

Bibliography

Beam, J. (1986) *In the Life: A Black Gay Anthology*, Alyson Publications.
Bosche, S. (1983) *Jenny Lives with Eric and Martin*, Gay Men's Press.
Mokin, L. (1979) *One Foot on the Mountain*: An Anthology of British Feminist Poetry 1969–1979, Only Women Press.
Rich, A. (1980) *On Lies, Secrets and Silence*: Selected Prose 1966–1978, Virago.
GLC Industry and Employment Branch 'Danger: Heterosexism at Work'.
GLC Working Party (1985) 'Changing the World', A London Charter for Gay and Lesbian Rights.
ILEA Relationships & Sexuality Project and Resources Group (1986) 'Positive Images' Materiography. Series No. 11, April, Pub. Learning Resources Branch.
Teaching London Kids. Article No. 23 available from 20 Durham Road, London SW20.

CHAPTER 9

'A word might slip and that would be it.' Lesbian Mothers and Their Children

LESBIAN MOTHERS GROUP

Lesbian mothers who have managed to get custody of their children after divorce are already familiar with the level of denial and subterfuge there has to be to win their custody case, and the anguish this entails. The law is punitive towards lesbian mothers and will award custody to the father if possible. If the mother manages to keep her children other battles remain. Once children go to school they are often in an atmosphere where 'lesbian' is a term of abuse.

In some areas lesbian women have come together to form support groups and this chapter is based on a discussion in a lesbian mothers group in 1987. The group had started meeting a few years before as a feminist motherhood group.

Joan, who is a founder member of the group, writes: 'We had met through the local women's centre and the impetus to start a group came from a desire to share our joys and our problems in a supportive environment. Soon it transpired that the core attenders were all lesbian and it was decided to continue with that as a central feature of the group. One of the original aims was to keep the group open so that women new to the area or new to lesbian motherhood could join and draw on support.

'Another important aspect of the group has been to organize social occasions when our children could meet one another and thus discover there are other children in a similar position. This has meant that women who are not "out" to their children do not join the group. There are many reasons why women do not come "out". However, there is a real need for another group to support women in this situation.

'This chapter is based on a transcript of a discussion in which the group considered some issues about how, as lesbian mothers, we support our children to survive in schools where the atmosphere is not only strongly heterosexual but possibly also overtly hostile to lesbianism and homosexuality.'

In the playground

The day before this discussion Joan's seven-year-old daughter, Miranda, had been called 'a lezzie' in the playground.

> *Joan*: . . . this little boy went past and called Miranda a 'lezzie'. She called him 'gay'. He kicked her.

This raised a number of issues for Joan, and later for the group, about how to support children in school and how they cope with comments about lesbianism. Joan discussed it with Miranda and pointed out that 'lesbian is a word, not a term of abuse'. However, deeper issues are more difficult to resolve. These issues may include feeling different from other pupils because of having a lesbian mother as well as coping with any abuse which may be hurled knowingly or unknowingly by other pupils:

> *Joan*: The deeper issue is to do with being the daughter of a lesbian mother. For children of lesbian mothers who don't feel they can cope with it, and don't have friends who will support them it may be difficult.

'Do your children know about you?'

It is all these kinds of pressures which have made it hard for us and may stop other women from being open with their children about lesbianism. Brenda has not yet told her children.

> *Joan* (to Brenda): Do your children know about you?
> *Brenda:* Well no, mine don't know. They would just see me and Sue as best friends and my sons are so young. They don't notice anything even under their noses. But my daughter Ruthie is eight. She just thinks that we're very good friends.
> *Sue:* Well she's very thoughtful about it, Ruthie . . . But it's quite new to them and it's gradual. It will be quite a gradual realization.

Among our group, Brenda, Sarah, Sue and Liz all have sons. Whether or not to tell them and how to do it has caused some anxiety.

> *Brenda*: I think for me it's going to be much more difficult with my sons when they reach an age rather than my daughter. Now I already feel they're very different species in so many respects.

Sarah's ex-husband told her sons.

> *Sarah*: My sons are twenty-three and twenty-one and I didn't actually tell them, but my ex-husband did.
> *Sue*: How did they react to that?
> *Sarah*: I felt I should have told them and I was prepared to tell them, but I'd never actually done it. He took it upon himself to do it and therefore put his biased point of view but it doesn't seem to have affected them at all in their relationship with me, and I've since talked to them about it. I certainly found it more difficult to tell the boys than to talk to Ann about it.

When Liz told her children, her daughter then aged ten was very upset. Her son who was then thirteen accepted it and has now told one or two friends.

> *Liz*: I told my children about three years ago when I didn't have a relationship. I deliberately sat them down and told them, and David knew more or less anyway and said 'fine'. Noelle ran away and cried for about two hours but it was really only theory to them because I didn't have a relationship for about eighteen months after that. Now David has told a couple of his friends. He tested it out on his best friend and heaved a sigh of relief when he was still spoken to.

'I don't think I'll tell anybody at school'

None of our children have discussed lesbianism at school. Joan says that Miranda has learned very quickly that lesbianism is not a subject to be mentioned in the classroom.

> *Joan*: I decided not to warn Miranda to be careful who she talked to about lesbianism. I decided it was a bad thing to give her negative ideas. But she chose herself not to tell anybody at school. She knew instinctively or by experience that you don't go round saying, 'My Mum's a lesbian.'

We know it is difficult to be different in any way at school although some differences are accepted and even valued. Others are not.

Sarah: To be different in any way is to be the odd one out at school. You have to be the same as everybody else.

Joan: But it depends what kind of difference. There is a Russian girl in Miranda's class who comes to school and tells her friend. 'My mother is a Russian Princess.' Miranda doesn't go to school and say, 'My mother is a lesbian.' They know what scores points and what's going to give them a bad time.

However, Miranda has recently discussed lesbianism with her best friend Zina. Zina saw some graffiti on the wall about lesbians and this gave them a chance to discuss it.

Joan: Miranda recently came out to her best friend Zina about me. Zina was really supportive to Miranda. They were talking about the graffiti written on the wall about lesbians and Zina said, 'What is a lesbian?' Her mother explained to her it's women loving women. Zina's face just lit up and she said to Miranda, 'Oh can we be lesbians when we grow up?' Which is really nice, so I think that Miranda feels quite safe there is certainly one person that she can rely on, but to what extent I don't know.

Ann has made a decision not to tell friends at school.

Sarah: The first thing Ann said to me when I told her was: 'I don't think I'll tell anybody at school. You were, what, nine?'

Ann: Yes.

Sarah: I didn't say, 'Don't tell anybody,' but that's their safety.

Liz is sure neither of her children would discuss lesbianism at school.

Liz: I don't think David would tell people at school, I really don't, and Noelle seems petrified that anyone would find out.

Concerned about the repercussions, Sue has warned her son not to openly discuss her lesbianism.

Sue: My children didn't go to school and tell anybody else and I think I told my youngest one that he ought to be careful about spreading it around because he was so unaware that there was anything wrong about it. Quite unaware.

This was part of Joan's concern for Miranda.

Joan: I think that's what I felt about Miranda. That she would let herself in for something – that she wouldn't realize the implications. Because she'd been surrounded by people who thought positively about it, it would be a real shock to come up against a negative, or even worse, a hostile response.

'I realized I shouldn't expect Noelle to fight my battles'

In school none of our children draw attention to having a mother who is a lesbian because it is not a safe environment. For the same reason if our children were challenged at school about their mother's lesbianism, most would deny it. In a contradictory way, knowing this can be rather hurtful. It is hard to accept that our children would deny the truth when we have struggled to reach a position where we are happy to be open about lesbianism. However, in time, most of us have come to see the children's denial as a survival strategy for them.

Ann goes to a large comprehensive school. How would she cope if she was challenged at school?

> *Joan*: Would you deny it?
> *Ann*: I don't really know. I suppose if it got out and everybody knew, I think because I'd be in the minority I'd deny it. If people in my class knew I'd probably just not say anything. It would be embarrassing because if I say to one person, 'Yes that is true,' and then they went and told another and another and it would just go round. So if one person came up and asked me, 'Is this rumour true?' I'd probably say 'No' or say 'go away' or something. Because I wouldn't want it to get out. I'd feel uncomfortable.

Initially Liz was hurt when her daughter Noelle also said that she would deny that her mother is a lesbian. However, on reflection Liz has come to understand how Noelle has a right to make her own decision.

> *Liz*: When I asked Noelle [now age 13] what she would say if anybody asked her about me she said she would deny it. I was very very hurt. I talked it over with Cath (a lesbian and a close friend). She said her son . . . had got into a fight at school (about her) and had come home really upset . . . She told him that she didn't expect him to fight her battles for her. . . . That was fine by her and that really helped me because I realized I shouldn't expect Noelle to fight my battles either.
> *Sarah*: Anyway it is our issue and not theirs.

Liz told her children that they could deny it, if they were challenged.

> *Liz*: I actually did tell my children that if they want to deny it that's fine and I think that helped them because they were caught a bit between loyalties.
> *Joan*: I've not faced that as an issue. I suppose it's only just come up because of what happened yesterday. I suppose I would be hurt if

Miranda denied it and I think probably I do need to work out whether I could let her off that divided loyalty hook. It's something that I need to look at.

Brenda: Well they'll fight what battles they can, won't they?

'I used to think I was the only one'

Getting to know other children with lesbian mothers can be a great support for children and this is a major aspect of this group.

> *Joan*: One of the main aims of the group is to get the children together so that they do know other children in a similar position.

Ann feels easier because her mother is a member of this group.

> *Ann*: When I didn't know Mum came to a lesbian mothers' group I used to think I was the only one. I'd be one person on my own, nobody I could really trust. Now there are people like Noelle I can talk to and not be embarrassed or not feel like I'm keeping a big secret, because we don't have to hide anything. If I'm talking to other friends I have to be consciously thinking about what to say because a word might slip and that would be it. Here you can say almost whatever you like because you don't have to be worried about a word slipping out or saying something that will go round the school.
> *Sue*: Doesn't that sound familiar? It does to me. As an adult lesbian in the wrong company – the company of people who don't know; it is exactly the same thing isn't it?

Joan reminds us that fears about losing their children terrorize many lesbian mothers.

> *Joan*: There are quite a lot of lesbian mothers at the school who are not able for reasons usually to do with custody to be out to their children and I think that's a big dividing line. As far as this group goes all the people are out to their children and there aren't that many custody hassles. That makes a difference. I'm sure that there could be another group where the main problem of those mothers would be to do with custody.

'All that cultural hate'

Many of us believe that feminism is a major challenge to male ideas. We have often found that our sons have resisted ideas about feminism very strongly whereas they have managed to come to terms with lesbianism.

> *Sarah*: 'Lesbianism' they think: 'oh well they can get on with that,' and it doesn't affect men really, but our feminism does.
> *Brenda*: Because you're asking them to change their attitudes and ideas.
> *Brenda*: To look at themselves.
> *Angela*: Just that little let up on the chauvinism would make such a difference. What do you think about that Ann?

Ann is not hopeful. She thinks most boys like tormenting girls.

> *Ann*: I don't think boys at school want to be non-sexist. They find it rather fun being sexist because they say, 'Oh let's go and push the girls about. Let's go and hit the girls.' It's something for them to do almost. If they're bored they can go and make stupid remarks at girls. Actually there are two boys who are really nice and if they even sit on the table with girls they're meant to be 'going out' with the girls. It is so difficult.
> *Sarah*: Just to be friends.

Ann had a friend called Tom in her junior school. Now she really misses his friendship.

> *Ann*: In my old school there was this really nice boy called Tom. He was a bit of a loud mouth but I liked him. I never noticed until just lately what a loss it is not to be able to speak to boys. I used to be able to really talk to him and nobody mentioned or talked about it. It used to be nice to be able to speak to them as if they're just . . .
> *Brenda*: People?
> *Ann*: Yes, but now it's not done. It's boys and girls. You suddenly realize that one minute you've got to like boys, the next minute you've got to hate them. You're stuck, you're lost. You just don't know where you are.
> *Brenda*: It's weird isn't it? This tension is set up.
> *Joan*: This little boy that called Miranda 'a lezzie,' I suggested to her that one way to deal with that was to invite him home to tea. She was just horrified, and yet when she's had problems with girls in her class that's how we've dealt with it. We've invited them home to tea and tried to sort it out. When I tried to do that with this boy she said 'Oh no'. So there are different rules that apply.
> *Sue*: So destructive isn't it?
> *Sarah*: It makes you wonder how any man and woman ever have a decent relationship in the end when there's so much hatred.
> *Sue*: Makes you realize why so few do actually.

Angela: And why it's all so fraught.

Sarah: Because you've got to get over all that cultural hate.

Postscript

Although no one in the group has had awful custody struggles we have all had our bad moments and the odd crisis. We do realize, however, that for many women the fight to keep their children is the central struggle in their lives. For this reason we are donating the money from this chapter to the Rights of Women Custody Campaign. The legal establishment of the rights of lesbian mothers will mean that the positive experiences of the women in this group regarding openness and support will be a possibility for all lesbian mothers.

Thanks to Liz, Sue, Brenda, Angela, Joan, Sarah and Ann for taking part in this discussion.

CHAPTER 10

The Sexual Harassment of Young Women

JACQUI HALSON

Introduction

This chapter focuses on one important aspect of the collective experience of young women – sexual harassment. The discussion is based on information gathered as part of a broader research project on gender, sexuality and power.[1] The young women whose experiences are described here were fourteen years old at the time of the study.[2] All were white, working and lower-middle-class students attending a co-education school which I call Henry James Comprehensive.[3] I spent nine months in the school as a researcher. I attended classes with students, conducted recorded interviews, spent time observing them at leisure and in school and, of course, made copious notes.

The chapter is divided into three sections. In the first section, I discuss what sexual harassment is and identify the forms it may take. In the second I describe in some detail the young women's experiences of sexual harassment, first, by 'Casanova' teachers, second, by lads whom they know, and note the impact of these experiences on their lives. A short concluding section argues that although sexual harassment is a form of violence commonly experienced by young women, schools sanction it – largely by non-intervention – and so help to reproduce, rather than challenge, existing imbalances of power between women and men.

What is sexual harassment?

Less than a decade ago, the phrase sexual harassment was almost unknown in Britain although the behaviour it describes is far from new. During the 1980s there has been a growing awareness that sexual harassment is a widespread problem (Hadjipotiou 1983) but until recently it was defined as a working woman's issue. The term covers any 'repeated and unwanted comments, looks, suggestions or physical contact that might threaten a woman's job security or create a stressful or intimidating working environment' (Sedley and Benn 1982, p. 6). In the USA and Australia, where the severity and extent of the problem is recognized, legislation exists which specifically prohibits sexual harassment, compensates victims and brings sanctions against employers. In Britain, a few cases involving sexual harassment have been brought to Industrial Tribunals and a few trade unions have campaigned on the issue, regarding it both as a sex discrimination and a health and safety issue.[4]

Limited as these developments have been in Britain, there is a small body of literature (trade union guide-lines, books and pamphlets, articles in newspapers and popular women's magazines) as well as TV films which have served to publicize the issue. Carole Jones (1984) and Pat Mahony (1985) have both written about sexual harassment in schools but there is very little other writing on this subject and very little public debate about the problems faced by younger women and girls in mixed schools or about sexual harassment in other non-work contexts (see Hey 1986; Wise and Stanley 1981). The issues are not quite the same because a woman's job security is not threatened when sexual harassment occurs in non-work situations. Nevertheless sexual harassment is a problem for women and girls wherever it occurs. It creates a stressful and intimidating general environment.

Sexual harassment or 'just larking about'?

Sexual harassment can take many forms. It may involve physical contact as, for example, when a girl/woman is patted, stroked, hugged or held against her will. Being pinched, squeezed, grabbed, groped and more serious sexual assaults also constitute sexual harassment. It does not always involve contact, however. Sexual harassment may be verbal or 'psychological': staring, leering, 'standing too close for comfort', being followed, threatening body postures, sexual remarks or taunting, obscene gestures or jokes, explicit conversations about sex which cause offence as well as subtle or explicit pressure for sexual activity.

Some of the more common forms of sexual harassment are often trivialized or dismissed as 'inoffensive' or 'friendly': 'just teasing' or 'just larking about'. Drawing the line between acceptable and unacceptable behaviour is not always easy. As Mary Bularzik (1978, p. 4) argues, 'there is a thin line between harassment and teasing'. However, the important question is: Who draws the line? Who is allowed to define for herself what is or is not offensive? In schools, on the streets and in workplaces, women and men joke, tease each other, flirt and 'lark about'. Sometimes these exchanges are mutual and cause no offence or embarrassment to anyone. What distinguishes sexual harassment from friendly sexual banter or flirtation is that it is not mutual; it is not welcome; it offends; it threatens. Sexual harassment, to paraphrase Lin Farley (1978, p. 14), is non-reciprocal, unsolicited masculine behaviour which asserts a girl's or woman's sexual identity over her identity as a person.[5] Although such behaviour is often thought to be 'about sexual attraction', it is primarily about men exercising power over women.

Experiencing sexual harassment

The young women of Henry James School suffer sexual harassment from the different groups of men and boys with whom they come into contact but the severity of the abuse varies. They are exposed to sexual harassment on the street, and in other public places, by strangers. Many of the young women I spoke to had been followed – on foot and in cars; subjected to unwelcome and intimidating comments; they had been 'flashed' at. These experiences induce very real fear. However, although several girls described incidents involving strangers, by far the majority of the incidents described involved people they knew, and they are especially vulnerable in their mixed school. At school they are harassed by teachers and other 'trusted' adults and they face harassment in school and out of school from lads – both older and younger – whom they know.

'Casanova' teachers

Before any of the girls talked frankly to me about one of their teachers – a man whom I shall call Mr Ryder – I had met him several times and interviewed him once. I had told him – and other teachers – that I was not studying teacher/pupil interactions. I explained that I was 'doing research on how the kids get on with each other'. This was true: my focus was on the girls' and boys' experiences of gender and on their interactions with one another. Some teachers understandably reacted with apprehension to my presence in the school. Mr Ryder seemed to have particular cause for concern, however. He accused me – albeit jokingly – of being 'a spy for the Head' and asked me a couple of times in passing, 'How's the world of spying going?'

As the girls took me into their confidence, I began to understand why Mr Ryder was worried about my investigations. During an interview with three girls, when the conversation turned to subjects and teachers, I simply asked if anyone had Mr Ryder as a teacher. Lynn immediately exclaimed, 'No, Oh! Not him!' and the girls laughed. 'Why d'you say that?' I asked. 'What's wrong with Mr Ryder?' There was a short pause:[6]

> *Lynn*: Well, when I was in [the lesson] he just kept lookin' at me all the time and it was *embarrassing*!
> *Interviewer*: Really? . . . Lookin' at your face or –
> *Lynn*: No!
> *Interviewer*: Lookin' you up and down?
> *Lynn*: Yeah! It's *embarrassing*!

I put the same question to other girls and received similarly immediate and emphatic responses:

> *Pauline*: Yeah! He's a right Casanova. I hate him.
> *Interviewer*: Why d'you say he's a Casanova?
> *Pauline*: It's the way he sits on the table with his legs up. It's just the way he sits there, lying down with his feet on the table, givin' you really sly smiles. It really bugs me!
> *Liz*: . . . he sort of put his arm round me . . . I don't think he meant it but I didn't like it.
> *Pauline*: Makes you feel a bit . . . uneasy.
> *Liz*: It shocked me a bit.

Liz's phrase, 'I don't think he meant it', neatly captures one of the dilemmas or uncertainties the girls face in defining such behaviour as sexual harassment: it is so 'normal'. It is ordinary, everyday behaviour. It conforms to what is widely considered 'normal' in mixed-sex interactions. Although it is clearly inappropriate given the nature of the relationship here – that of teacher and student – it is commonplace masculine behaviour, behaviour which makes those on the receiving end – women and girls – feel uncomfortable and threatened. Mr Ryder behaves as if the girls were present in school for his benefit or for his entertainment rather than for their education. Given his status as a teacher the girls are not in a realistic position to challenge his behaviour. They cannot tell him to 'get lost'. 'As soon as you see Mr Ryder you think "oh dear". You don't say anything,' Fiona said. Like the boss at work, the 'Casanova' teacher has a captive audience.

Despite their relative powerlessness, however, the girls use such resources as they have to help one another 'cope' with teachers who sexually harass them. Their resources are each other, the 'grapevine' and the rumours that pass along it from one group of girls to another: 'people tell you to watch out for him.' As far as I can be certain, the rumours about particular teachers 'having sex with a girl' or 'keeping a girl in after school and . . .' are just rumours.[7] They serve the very useful function of warning new girls what they might expect from particular men. They help the girls define which teachers they can trust and which they cannot trust. This does not prevent them from being sexually harassed but it at least forewarns them about the possibility. It publicizes teachers' inappropriate and offensive behaviour amongst the girls, giving them a shared, collective definition of 'problem men'. 'It makes you think what teachers are like when you're on your own with them,' according to Liz.

Mr Ryder has been selected for discussion here because the girls singled him out as a particularly offensive character. As Fiona said, 'He's the worst one,' and Lorna agreed, adding, 'There's a teacher like that in every school.' Some teachers behave towards young women students in ways which are less blatant than Mr Ryder's approach; nevertheless they embarrass the girls. In one classroom I observed a girl and a boy 'fighting' over a ruler. The girl was trying to retrieve the ruler which the boy had borrowed. The boy was holding it at arm's length. The teacher had not observed the cause of the dispute; he simply became aware that a dispute was ongoing. He responded by saying, 'Put him down, Karen!' causing a guffaw of laughter. Karen was one of only two girls in a Design and Technology (DT) class. She was immediately silenced. She blushed and lowered her eyes in embarrassment. Another girl told me that when she asked for a screw in another DT class, a teacher is reputed to have replied, 'See me after school and I'll give you one.' Remarks of this kind are, arguably, so trivial that they merit no concern. The fact that they are commonplace does not mean that they are unimportant. They are significant in that they cause embarrassment and they contribute to the maintenance of gender difference by 'sexualizing' situations at women's expense.

In classrooms where girls are in a minority, the effects of such harassment compound girls' alienation from subjects like Design and Technology which are traditionally masculine. At Henry James School, DT is compulsory for all second- and third-form students. Thereafter, it is optional and attracts a small minority of young women students. There are many factors which influence option choices. Having a man teacher who is well known throughout the school (at least amongst the girls) for sexual harassment is one factor. Asked if she enjoyed the subject, Lynn said, 'Yes.' Then she added, 'If I had him [Mr Ryder], I think I'd drop out.'

Mr Ryder knows that, as a teacher (not as a man), his behaviour is unwarranted; hence, I suspect, his concern about my 'spying'. Although it does not stop him entirely, his behaviour is restricted by a professional code of ethics. He harasses the girls in ways which (as far as I can be certain) do not breach that code. He is subtle. Other boys and men with whom the girls come into contact have no such code and few inhibitions in their treatment of the girls. They are not so subtle.

Being 'got' by lads you know

Many of the girls I spoke with have experienced what they call being 'got'. This involves one or more of the following: being chased, being grabbed or groped, being pushed to the ground, pinned down or sat upon, being sexually assaulted. Often, these physical assaults are preceded by leering and accompanied by verbal sexual harassment.

The assaults are usually perpetrated by lads whom the girls know; they occur with regularity, often in the street, sometimes in or around their own or friends' houses. I use here the accounts of Liz and Pauline to illustrate what being 'got' entails. These accounts have been selected not because they are exceptional but because I had quite detailed discussions with these girls about their experiences. Without exception, every girl I interviewed more than once had had at least one similar experience.

Liz describes an incident which involved herself and two lads (aged about 16) whom she knows 'really well':

Liz: They got me on the floor 'n' everything. Eugh! I hated it!
Interviewer: What did they do?
Liz: They just sat on me and pulled my skirt up 'n' all that. An' it was horrible cos I was right in the middle of the street. But you can't do nothin' about it.

The next incident happened to Pauline when she was at her friend's house. Her friend's brother 'had all his mates in as well'. The lads 'got' her on the grass. What shocked her most was 'when it was Pamela's brother that got his hand up me – tried to get his hand up me. It really shook me up that did.'

On another occasion Liz went with a girlfriend to give a birthday card to a lad she knew who was having a party. The two girls were invited in and found they were the only girls. There were about twelve lads. Almost immediately the lads:

> Liz: . . . were all on top o' me, trying to get me knickers down 'n' everything. I hated it. I was screamin', kickin' everybody. Can't do nothin' about it. . . . They didn't properly get 'em down . . . cos I was kickin' everywhere. I just blew! They were teasing me about it at school 'n' everything.
> Interviewer: Who teased you? The boys that had done it?
> Liz: Yeah.
> Interviewer: What were they saying afterwards?
> Liz: Calling me 'knickers'. Things like that.

The first and most obvious point to be made is that these accounts of being 'got' are descriptions of some of the cruder, more obviously violent manifestations of sexual harassment. This behaviour asserts the girls' sexual identity with complete disregard for their autonomy as human beings. It is behaviour which stops short of rape usually but not always. One of the young women in my study was raped when she was thirteen years old by three fifteen-year-old boys whom she knew. Just as the line between teasing and sexual harassment is not easy to draw, a fine line exists between rape and the sexual assaults experienced by girls on a more day-to-day basis. Whether or not rape actually occurs, the fear or threat of rape exists on many of the occasions when girls are 'got' by lads they know. Assaults of the kind described here are not rare occurrences. These are incidents which the girls suffer repeatedly, creating for them a humiliating and threatening environment. Whereas Mr Ryder's behaviour caused the girls some discomfort or embarrassment, the lads they know cause them acute humiliation: this behaviour horrifies them.

Secondly, it is important to note that these experiences contribute to, and reinforce, girls' sense of powerlessness. Talking with many young women over a period of nine months, I often heard phrases like, 'I couldn't control 'em,' 'I didn't know what to do,' or Liz's 'you can't do nothin' about it.' The girls are not passive victims of these assaults but they are, as individuals, in a very real sense, powerless to stop the lads in mid-assault and powerless to prevent them from occurring. Pauline relied on the lads themselves to stop assaulting her when they decided they were 'going too far' or when they decided they had had enough. In Liz's case, all the screaming and kicking she described did not in itself stop the lads. The older brother of the one whose party it was 'came in and stopped it in the end'. One fourteen-year-old girl is no match for a gang of fourteen-year-old lads. Sexual harassment of individual girls by groups of lads is one of the most vivid illustrations of the exercise of collective male power.

One of the strategies which girls adopt in an attempt to protect themselves from assault is to police their *own* behaviour. Another girl – Tracy – told me that she had opted out of the short cut to her friend's house because of repeated harassment by gangs of young boys en route: 'I make sure they don't come round me cos I go the long way.' This is one of the very obvious ways in which sexual harassment controls girls' lives. It affects where they feel they can, with safety, walk alone. Such 'avoidance strategies' are one of the few perceived alternatives available to the girls but they do not ultimately protect them from assault, even where such strategies are practicable, because the responsibility for sexual harassment is not theirs: whichever route they take, wherever they go, whatever they wear, they risk being sexually harassed, and they are sexually harassed.

Schools and 'normalization'

The experiences of sexual harassment described so far by Liz and Pauline are experiences which occurred outside school. School and 'life' are not discrete categories, however. 'Schools are reflections of society,' as the Headmaster of Henry James School once said to me. One of the ways in which boys learn about and practise their masculine behaviour – including sexual harassment – is in interaction with others in schools.

Lindsey is convinced that her five-year-old brother first learned about sexual harassment when he went to school:

> *Tracy*: I was standin' in the garden, playing ball and he (Lindsey's brother) came up behind me and put his hand up my skirt! I felt really silly!
> *Lindsey*: I think he gets it from school. He's only started doin' it since he started school.
> *Interviewer*: Does he do it to you?

Lindsey: Yeah! I smack him though. He don't do it [to me] no more. He used to. When he first started school he were terrible – really dirty.

Interviewer: And he's only five? And he's picked that up from school?

Lindsey: He must've done cos he never did it before.

At secondary school the boys continue to be 'terrible'. Sexual harassment by boys occurs with regularity though less often in the more 'obvious' or more brutal forms described by the girls earlier. Verbal sexual harassment, however, and some of the less brutal forms of contact harassment are as common in school as they are on the streets. Frequently the lads who assault the girls on the street or at home or at parties are the same lads they know in school, as was the case with Liz, taunted by the comments 'knickers'. This served to remind her of the humiliation and fear she experienced at the time of the assault, to embarrass her further by making her humiliation more public and to reinforce her status – in the lads' eyes – as a sexual object. Such name calling threatens (further) violence. The lads have assaulted her once, their verbal abuse reminds her that they could – and probably will – do it again.

Other names with which the girls are taunted include 'lez' (lesbian) 'bitch' and 'dog'. Girls are habitually referred to as 'slags' or one of its equivalents. The effect of such labelling can be profound (see Lees 1986). Other remarks, such as 'Look at the tits on that' or 'It's got a nice arse', are common. Here, impersonal pronouns (that, it) replace personal pronouns (her, she) when the referent is female in addition to reference being made to a dissected portion of her body.

Boys comment on girls' appearance: 'nice jumper' (leering at breasts); 'nice skirt' (leering at buttocks or legs). They point out that a bra strap is showing or make comments or jokes about periods or Tampax to embarrass the girls. They slide fingers down the girls' backs, they pretend to, attempt to or do lift the girls' skirts. Girls are leered at in classrooms and corridors, 'felt up' or groped as they walk about. Sometimes they have little opportunity to retaliate because they do not know who assaulted them. In one such case, a young woman was walking up a crowded staircase en route to an afternoon lesson. She was groped suddenly by someone behind her, his hand resting firmly though momentarily on her crotch. She turned round immediately, her face a mixture of shock, anger and embarrassment but she could not identify the guilty boy, there being several in the immediate vicinity. She muttered 'bastard' and continued upstairs. On many occasions the girls do know who is responsible and they are in a relatively 'safe' environment but they make no obvious response. They appear to ignore the incident and often it is assumed that girls find being 'felt up' or being commented upon complimentary. They do not find it flattering or funny; at worst they find it humiliating and offensive, at best they find it boring and stupid:

> *Fiona*: There was these two fifth formers behind me. One of them just came up behind me and felt my bum! They were makin' comments like 'Hasn't she got a lovely arse!' . . . But I didn't take any notice of it.
> *Interviewer*: Yeah. How did you – can you describe how you felt when they felt your bum and when they were callin' names and –
> *Fiona*: Oh God!
> *Interviewer*: Did you feel flattered?
> *Fiona*: No! I just thought, 'oh, they're being stupid again'. I just walked off.

In a sense the girls are 'forced' to 'ignore' sexual harassment, to accept the 'inevitability' of it because the world in which they live – their school, this society – does not empower them to challenge boys'/men's behaviour. It is as if there is a war going on and the girls have no ammunition with which to respond to the violence they suffer from men and boys. Just as it never occurred to the girls in Sue Lees' (1986) study to say, 'How *dare* they call us slags,' it never seemed to occur to the young women in my study to say, 'How *dare* they assault us.' All they say is, 'it's horrible'; 'it's embarrassing'; 'I don't care. I've got over it now'; 'you can't do nothin' about it'. In the face of such violence, young women have to be helped – or empowered – to fight back.

With a few exceptions (see Mahony 1985) schools do nothing which could be regarded as a serious attempt to address the problem of sexual harassment of young women. There is a sense in which 'everyone knows it goes on' and some – particularly women teachers – are only too aware of the difficulties they and the young women students face (see Whitbread 1980). In general though, schools sanction rather than challenge sexual harassment. Whilst most schools have policies on 'ordinary' violence, few have policies on sexual violence. Whilst smoking, wearing denim clothes and boys' wearing ear-rings are regarded as inappropriate behaviour for students at Henry James School, calling girls slags, for example, is not. Sexual harassment is not generally recognized as a problem which merits intervention and so it largely remains 'hidden' from or ignored by those who could intervene on the girls' behalf, by those who could at least try to 're-educate' the boys into attitudes and patterns of behaviour which are not contemptuous of and violent toward women.

Where instances of sexual harassment do come to the attention of teachers, they are likely to be trivialized or dismissed. The following account illustrates the lack of seriousness with which one senior member of staff at Henry James School regarded an incident which in my view constituted sexual harassment and which clearly offended and upset the young woman concerned. I had spent only a few days in the school when some graffiti appeared on one of the playground walls. It read 'MARY IS A SLAG' and was painted in large white letters. The graffiti – and Mary – became the subject of much gossip. One of the senior members of staff told me that Mary's mother was 'threatening action' unless something was done about the incident. He commented to me, casually and quite unselfconsciously:

> I don't think she realizes that 'slag' is a very common term of abuse. It doesn't have the overtones of prostitution that it used to have. It seems to have replaced 'cow'.

In a sense the teacher is correct: 'slag' is just one of the long list of words which are used to describe and condemn women – and only women. However, he implies that Mary's mother is 'over-reacting'; he trivializes the incident. He was non-committal when he mentioned that Mary was 'a bit upset'. Her friends, with whom I later discussed the issue, described the 'floods of tears' that Mary had shed, both because of the writing on the wall and because of the way in which similar bits of graffiti subsequently appeared on walls and desks throughout the school. There was no public condemnation of the incident. The violation of a young woman's autonomy was not taken seriously by the senior member of staff.

Challenging sexual harassment: empowering women

Young women suffer sexual harassment from strangers, teachers, adult family members, brothers, 'friends' and acquaintances in and out of school. These are individuals of diverse ages and different statuses relative to the girls. The only thing which these individuals have in common is that they are *masculine*. Interactions between women and men do not take place in a vacuum, or 'spontaneously' or 'naturally'. They are learned in complex ways; they are socially constructed, albeit on a biological base. The interactions described in this chapter are both a product of and a reproduction of power differences between women and men. They are based on different attitudes toward women's and men's bodies and different ideas about women's and men's bodies and different ideas about women's and men's sexuality. They constitute sexual violence.

Schools, as the Headmaster said, are 'reflections of society'. They help to reproduce rather than to change the imbalance of power between women and men in various ways, not least by failing to recognize the extent to which young women are subjected to sexual harassment, by failing to note the significant impact which these experiences have on their lives and personalities, by failing to intervene. In these circumstances, young women cope as best they can in the full and certain knowledge that many of the boys and men with whom they come into contact behave with disrespect, contempt and violence towards them, and that this is considered 'normal'. Mandy sums up her fourteen years' experience of being a young woman in a man's world thus:

Who doesn't treat you like shit? I mean, come on. Tell me.

Mandy and other young women have a right to be treated with respect. Schools, in my view, have a duty to do all within their power to challenge and condemn boys' and men's sexual violence and, thereby, to help empower young women to challenge and change their world.

Acknowledgements

I should like to thank the people who have taken the time and effort to comment on the first draft of this chapter. In particular, credit is due to Terry Lovell and Bob Burgess, my supervisors, who have, since I met them in 1983, given me their unfailing support; also to Hilary Graham and Lesley Holly for their constructive criticism.

Notes

1   ESRC funded project, the fieldwork for which was conducted between September 1984 and July 1985. This chapter is a shortened version of a more 'analytical' chapter of a PhD thesis entitled 'Gendered Subjectivity, Coercion and Resistance: A Study of Teenagers in Transition', to be submitted to The University of Warwick, September 1988.
2   Given the difficulty of determining precisely when girls (children)

become women (adults) I use the terms girls and young women inter-
changeably to refer to the fourteen year olds.

3   In order to ensure the anonymity of those involved, all the names
used – of the school and of people – are pseudonyms.

4   For example, the National Association of Local Government Officers
and the National Association of Teachers in Further and Higher
Education.

5   Farley defines sexual harassment as 'unsolicited, non-reciprocal male
behaviour that asserts a woman's sex role over her function as a
worker'.

6   Transcript notation:
– indicates an unfinished sentence
. . . indicates that a word/phrase has been edited out usually because it
was repeated or 'non-essential'
A word in italics indicates that a particular emphasis was placed
upon it.
The spoken word is different from the written word. As far as
possible, words have been reproduced in print as they were spoken: cos
rather than because; 'em rather than them; y'know and d'you rather
than you know and do you; yer rather than you.

7   This is not to suggest that men teachers do not sexually abuse girl
students. I have no 'evidence' that the rumours were based on real events.

Bibliography

Bularzik, M. (1978) 'Sexual Harassment at the Workplace', *Radical
America*, Vol. 12, No. 4.

Farley, L. (1978) *Sexual Shakedown*, McGraw Hill Book Co., New York.

Hadjipotiou, N. (1983) *Women and Harassment at Work*, Pluto Press,
London.

Hey, V. (1986) *Patriarchy and Pub Culture*, Tavistock, London.

Jones, C. (1984) 'Sexual tyranny in mixed sex schools: an in-depth study of
male violence' in G. Weiner (ed.) *Just a Bunch of Girls: Feminist
approaches to schooling*, Open University Press, Milton Keynes.

Lees, S. (1986) *Losing Out*, Hutchinson, London.

Mahony, P. (1985) *Schools for the Boys? Co-education reassessed*,
Hutchinson, London.

Sedley, A. and Benn, M. (1982) *Sexual Harassment at Work*, NCCL Rights
for Women Unit, London.

Whitbread, A. (1980) 'Female Teachers are Women First: Sexual harassment at work' in D. Spender and E. Sarah (eds) *Learning to Lose*,
Women's Press, London.

Wise, S. and Stanley, L. (1981) *Georgie Porgie: Sexual harassment in everyday life*, Pandora Press, London.

Appendix: Useful References and Addresses

Organizations

The name of each organization is followed by a brief description of the focus of its works.

ALRA/A woman's right to choose campaign, 88 Islington High Street, London N1 8EG. Abortion and all related subjects.

Birth Control Trust, 27–35 Mortimer Street, London W1. Contraception; sterilization; abortion.

Body Positive, P O Box 493, West Kensington, London W14 0TF. Aims to help to mobilize the individual's own resources in responding to the challenge of HIV Virus and to end the isolation associated with HIV Virus.

The British Life Assurance Trust, The BLAT Centre, BMA House, Tavistock Square, London WC1H 9JP. Family planning; AIDS; child abuse; sex education; personal relationships.

British Pregnancy Advice Service, Austy Manor, Wootton Wawen, Solihull, West Midlands B95 6BX. Aims to promote educational research into pregnancy and the termination of pregnancy and their effects.

Brook Advisory Centres Education and Publications Unit, 24 Albert Street, Birmingham B4 7UD. Sex and personal relationships; unplanned pregnancy; contraception.

CMAC (Catholic Marriage Advisory Council) Clitherow House, 1 Blythe Mews, Blythe Road, London W14 0NW. Sexuality, relationships, marriage.

Childline Free Post 1111, London EC4BB. Tel 0800 1111. Help for children.

Children's Legal Centre, 20 Compton Terrace, London N1 2UN. Young people's rights.

Family and Youth Concern, Wicken, Milton Keynes MK19 6BU. Personal relationships, sex, marriage, abortion, STDs.

Family Planning Association (Education Unit), 78 New Oxford Street,

London W1N 7RJ. Training, education, and consultation for the helping professions.

Health Education Authority, 74 New Oxford Street, London WC1AH. A national resource for information, advice and guidance about health education.

Kidscape, 82 Brook Street, London W1Y 1YG. Tel 01 493 9845. Education and information for children about abuse.

LGCM (Lesbian and Gay Christian Movement), St Botolph's Church, Aldgate, London EC3N 1AB. Resources, positive images, youth groups, counselling.

Lesbian and Gay Youth Movement, BM/GYM, London WC1N 3X. Aims to help young people to realize the many forms sex can take.

LIFE, 118–120 Warwick Street, Leamington Spa, CV32 4QY. Pregnancy; foetal development, abortion.

National Abortion Campaign, Wesley House, 4 Wild Court, London WC2B 5AU.

NSPCC, 67 Saffron Hill, London EC1N 8RS. Tel 01 242 1626.

Pregnancy Advisory Service, 11–13 Charlotte Street, London W1P 1HD. Unplanned pregnancy, abortion.

Rape Crisis London. Tel 01 837 1600.

SPOD Association to Aid the Sexual and Personal Relationships of People with Disability, 286 Camden Road, London N70BJ. Sexuality and disability.

Terence Higgins Trust Ltd, 52–54 Grays Inn Road, London WC1X 8LT. Promoting awareness and understanding of problems relating to AIDS/ARC and HIV.

Welsh AIDS Campaign, PO Box 348, Cardiff CF1 4XL.

Youth Support, 30 Crystal Palace Park Road, London SE26. Sexuality; parenthood; sexual abuse; sexual decision making.

Resources

Breaking the silence, Lusia Films 1984, Cinema of Women, 27 Clerkenwell Close, London EC1R 0AT.

Church Education Media Project, College of St Mark and St John, Plymouth PL6 8BH. Production of educational material for school governors.

Consortium Resources for Severe Learning Difficulties, Jack Tizzard School, Finlay Street, London SW6 6HB. Material on menstruation.

ILEA Relationships and Sexuality Project and Resources Group, April 1986, 'Positive Images' Materiography, Series No. 11, ILEA Learning Resources Branch.

Learning Development Aids, Wisbech Cambridgeshire.

Mental Health Film Council, 380–384 Harrow Road, London W9 2HU. Audio-visual media include all aspects of sexuality.

Pictorial Charts Educational Trust, 27 Kirchen Road, West Ealing, London W13 0UD. Sex education in a social context.

See Red Women's Workshop, 90A Camberwell Road, Camberwell, London SE5. Posters with positive images of women; sex education.

The English Centre, Sutherland Street, London SW1.

Unlearning fear. Albany Videos, Douglas Way, London SE8 4AG. Tel 01 692 6322.

Books

Adams, C., Fay J. and Loreen-Martin J. (1987) *No is Not Enough; Helping Teenagers Avoid Sexual Assault*, Impact California.

Allen, I. (1987) *Education in Sex and Personal Relationships*, Policy Studies Institute.

Anon (1984) *Developing a School Policy on Sexual Abuse*, G.E.N.: an anti-sexist education magazine. Summer no. 3.

Cartledge and Ryan (1983) *New thoughts on Old Contradictions*, Women's Press.

Christopher, E. (1980) *Sexuality and Birth Control in Social and Community Work*, Temple Smith. Understanding different cultural attitudes and values.

Dworkin, A. (1987) *Intercourse*, Free Press.

Elliot, M. (1986) *Keeping safe. A practical guide to talking with children*, Bedford Square Press.

Elliot, M. (1986) *The Willow Street Kids: Its your Right to be Safe*, Bedford Square Press.

Farrell, C. (1978) *'My mother said': The way young people learned about sex and birth control*, Routledge and Kegan Paul.

Holt, A. and Randell, J. (1976) *The Two of Us*, Cambridge University Press. Investigates different kinds of relationships.

NSPCC *Protect Your Child from Sexual Assault. A Guide About Child Abuse for Parents*, NSPCC, 67 Saffron Hill, London EC1N 8RS.

Went, D. J. (1984) *Sex education: Some guidelines for teachers*, Bell and Hyman.

This list was compiled with the help of material from the National Children's Bureau and The Health Education Council among other sources.

Index